49

When Quiet Was the New Loud

Celebrating the Acoustic Airwaves
1998-2003

Tom Clayton

route

First published by Route in 2021
Pontefract, UK
info@route-online.com
www.route-online.com

ISBN: 978-1901927-84-9

First Edition

Tom Clayton asserts his moral
right to be identified as the author of this book

Cover Design:
John Sellards

Typeset in Bembo by Route

Printed & bound in Great Britain by TJ Books

For my parents

Introduction

> It's as if we panic-squeezed an entire imaginary generation
> of music in a gap between two decades. It was possibly some
> sort of pre-millennial defragging … we stripped everything
> right down before being beamed into the future.
>
> – Andy Votel

When I was about five years old, music arrived in my life in a startling
and upsetting way.

I don't remember much about my parents' old house. We moved
to a larger place shortly after this incident, when my little sister
arrived. What I *do* remember is the big stereo that took pride of
place in the living room. I was obsessed with its mysteries: what
were those tiny neon columns that danced whenever the music
played? Why wasn't I allowed to touch the turntable? And what on
earth did 'AUX IN' mean? On idle afternoons I would twiddle with
the controls to test the effects I could produce. Usually this would
involve accidentally uncovering obscure medium-wave radio stations
in different languages, or subjecting my poor parents' Chris Rea
cassettes to borderline obscene levels of bass. This time was different.
Having pushed a random series of buttons, then turned a few more
knobs just to be sure, I hit 'play'. The blaring result nearly knocked
me off my feet. One of the controls I'd messed with this time was
'master volume'; those neon columns formed a block. For what must
have only been a matter of seconds, the whole house seemed to shake
with noise, my young ears enduring a barrage of garbled static. I
scrabbled at the controls, desperately trying to work out which one
would stop the din. My dad rushed in and restored order, then turned
to scold me, before thinking better of it: my eyes were brimming
with tears. Those few cacophonous seconds were enough to instil
in me a lifelong suspicion of noise. It would be a long time before I
approached a stereo again.

Let's press play again: track one, side one, second one. It starts with a brief rumble, like a low-flying aeroplane. Then the sound shimmers and distorts, revealing itself as an effects-heavy guitar, each chord registering only in passing, like washes of rain on a windscreen. It is the riff that underpins 'Writing to Reach You', one of Travis' loveliest songs, and the opening number of their chart-conquering, seemingly inescapable second album, *The Man Who*.

That collection's domination of the late 1990s and early 2000s heralded the arrival of a brief, melancholy time in British music. It ran for roughly five years, from the end of 1998 until 2003, and was met with admiration and dismay as it unfolded. But what to call it? The word 'acoustic' seems to have stuck, but not much more. In his fine overview of the Britpop era, *The Last Party*, John Harris observes how its later years were overtaken by a 'vaguely troubled, ever-so-slightly millennial aesthetic that conveys very little of any meaning'. *NME* limply named it the 'New Acoustic Movement',[1] while Creation Records founder Alan McGee infamously put it in the bluntest of terms – labelling Coldplay's debut album *Parachutes* 'bedwetters' music' in a *Guardian* article previewing that year's Mercury Music Prize. As we'll see, it was rather more complicated – and a lot more creditable – than that.[2]

The biggest artists of the period – Travis, Coldplay and David Gray – experienced enormous, almost inconceivable success. More significantly, their best-known singles, 'Why Does It Always Rain On Me?', 'Yellow' and 'Babylon', are now part of the national songbook – radio staples still belted out by buskers and open-mic merchants to this day. Something about this trio of songs, and by extension, the acoustic era, clearly tapped into Britain's collective pre-millennial identity: vaguely-defined nostalgia, subdued wistfulness, quiet panic… call it what you will.

---

[1] It's worth stating from the off that the original incarnation of the New Acoustic Movement – the 'NAM' as many called it – only ever extended to a handful of bands. I've broadened its usage in this book for ease of referring to the artists mentioned within. You'll see them referred to as 'acoustic' – but most of them were anything but.

[2] McGee partially climbed down from his remark in an interview with the *Sunday Express* in March 2020, saying 'I do regret calling Coldplay bedwetters… a bit,' adding 'compared to what came after them, they were okay.'

The public embrace of this affable, homespun or otherwise 'authentic' music also reflected a retreat from a decade-long period of musical and social largesse which was rapidly beginning to sour. As *NME* put it in their 2018 piece reflecting on their own often-short-lived movements, the acoustic era was prompted by 'the likes of Noel Gallagher and Paul Weller deciding that the nineties had had its fun and it was time it went and sat on the Boring Stool to calm down'. By the late nineties, the leading lights of Britpop were releasing records that spoke of exhaustion with excess: Blur's grunge-indebted eponymous album of 1997, and its densely experimental follow-up, *13* (1999); Pulp's gloriously seedy *This Is Hardcore* (1998); Oasis' expansive, scattershot *Be Here Now* (1997). Suede, Supergrass and Catatonia, whose energy and intelligence had illuminated the decade, also produced similarly weary work. It was a time that felt – as Damon Albarn so acutely observed – like the death of a party. Daniel Rachel's brilliant oral history of Cool Britannia, *Don't Look Back in Anger*, contains a multitude of astute first-hand observations, some of which point towards the reasons for this collective slump. Steve Lamacq identifies the twin ghouls of commercialisation and overindulgence: 'By this point Britpop was everything from Radiohead to Ocean Colour Scene. It was huge and made no sense,' and later: 'cocaine killed Britpop ... people used it to make up for lack of ideas.' Contrast this lethargy with the confidence of 'Writing to Reach You', where Fran Healy casually works a mention of 'Wonderwall' into the first verse – a move which doesn't just cheekily own the fact the song shares a chord pattern with Oasis' behemoth, it knocks the idea of Britpop firmly into the past.[3] There was a cultural vacuum waiting to be filled – and following years of laddish belligerence, the time looked right for a more sensitive clutch of artists.

For much of the twentieth century, the appearance of an acoustic guitar on stage meant one of two things: you were about to hear a protest song, or you were about to hear a folk song. If you were really lucky, you might hear a combination of the two! In the late nineties a different sort of acoustic songwriting emerged. With Fran Healy spearheading the trend, it echoed both the cinematic

---

[3] The two bands were in fact great friends – and Oasis were key players in Travis' early career, as we'll see in the first chapter.

miserablism and cyber-paranoia of late-nineties masterpieces like The Verve's *Urban Hymns* and Radiohead's *OK Computer*, but subtly turned those qualities into something more grounded and relatable. Richard Ashcroft's and Thom Yorke's grandiose lyrics often found them grappling with man's place in the universe, and while Travis and co. never actively *dodged* those questions, theirs was ultimately a domestic arena – and it proved wildly successful. At the prospect of epochal change, Brits consumed the cultural equivalent of what we do best: putting the kettle on and griping about the weather.

The encroaching new millennium had a confusing effect on the UK. As the big '1' prepared to become a big '2', and Brits began to realise the significance of what was about to happen, we became increasingly reflective about ourselves. Our cultural output: TV, books, film, music and even public figures were subject to endless 'best of the millennium' debates, or packaged up in expansive shiny compilations. That 'end-of-year' feeling that critics know well – which prompts within us the need to list, to anthologise, to look back – was multiplied a hundred, even a thousand times over. The UK felt like it was scrambling for closure in the face of whatever was coming next – and for an already nostalgic country, it represented something close to a nervous breakdown. Suddenly we needed, somehow, to sum up our entire history. How could we demonstrate what we'd achieved, and show future generations what this one represented? It was always going to be an impossible task, demonstrated perfectly by the curatorial and financial struggles that dogged the Millennium Dome project throughout the late nineties.[4] But there was something else underpinning this desperate clamour for the past: we were ever so slightly scared of what was around the corner.

The 'Y2K Problem', popularly known as the Millennium Bug,[5] now considered merely a smirk-worthy footnote in the history

---

[4] Sushi bars and trapeze artists ended up figuring quite heavily, as I recall.

[5] In case you'd forgotten: the theory that, because many computer systems had only been designed to use the last two digits of the date format, the switch from '99 to '00 would effectively prompt computers to think they had been reset to the year 1900. As such, in the years leading up to the millennium there were fears of large-scale system reboots, fatal errors or otherwise terminal failures – and a corresponding global infrastructure meltdown. As it turned out, that didn't happen, prompting condemnation from many for causing 'unnecessary' panic. The army of IT professionals – whose unseen and largely unheralded efforts ensured The Bug was zapped – would probably argue otherwise.

books, was at the time deemed a major security threat, and had world leaders seriously worried; an estimated $300bn was ploughed into readying mainframes around the world. There was a maximalist feel to everything that happened in the run-up to 2000, like a season finale at full volume: in response to a wave of global paranoia that spread throughout 1999, the American Red Cross advised US citizens to have enough food and supplies on hand to endure 'disruptions of several days to a week' as New Year's Eve approached.[6] Religious cults crept back into the news, some of whom concluded that this numerical novelty meant the End of Days was upon us.

On a more earthly level, people were also beginning to realise that this 'internet' malarkey was really quite powerful indeed – and could be used for both good and sinister purposes. The way we thought about the so-called information superhighway was changing rapidly. It had gone from something you 'went on' for twenty minutes a day – after you'd cleared everyone off the landlines and endured several minutes of tortuous dial-up noises – to an increasingly indispensable way of life. The faster it grew, the more influence it gathered, and its far-reaching possibilities became clearer by the day. The internet was about to become the dominant means of communication, triggering an age of instant information which society was arguably ill-prepared for; we are still dealing with the ramifications today. Perhaps, then, our new-found taste for the comforting, wistful music of David Gray et al reflected the hesitancy we felt towards the impending challenges of a new century. It turned out we were right to be concerned.

★★★

These days, I have a naturally quiet voice – but it hasn't always been so. I gradually overcame my childhood fear of stereo speakers, and for most of my early years spent in the suburban outskirts of Bath I was a confident and outgoing kid. Barely a weekday evening went by when I wasn't involved in some kind of amateur dramatic show, choir performance, football match or Cub Scout meeting. On one occasion I hijacked an entire school assembly, performing an

---

[6] Although as it became clear the millennium would not herald anything much in the way of infrastructure collapse, John Koskinen, chairman of the President's Council on Year 2000 Conversion, admitted the biggest danger to life was now 'overreaction'.

extended impersonation of our exiting deputy head on his last day.[7] And though I suspected I wasn't the most tuneful of singers (my voice was often described, kindly, as 'powerful'), I led a loud and busy life all the same. Then the hormones kicked in, and the volume went down. Is it any wonder, then, that I identified with the quiet types as I began my musical journey? That I still do now? In telling the story of these albums, I'm also telling the tale of a kid who grew up loud, went quiet, and spent the best part of a decade trying to get his confidence back. And this music formed the soundtrack.

Briefly, it seemed, I had found my people: artists who didn't need to shout about how great they were to make a big impression on the listener. They knew the value of silence and stillness. They had also decided that, for better or worse, they didn't want to replicate the excesses of the previous decade. Theirs was an aesthetic that kicked against those polished visions of the future, thriving instead in gloomy, unkempt corners – in imperfection, fallibility and self-deprecation. Unlike their Britpop predecessors, or their New Rock inheritors, they weren't afraid to admit they felt inadequate, or scared, or unfashionable. They embraced their insecurities and made stirring, memorable music in the process of doing so.

I'm part of a generation whose formative musical years, covered by this book, are often thought of as either the epilogue to one era (Britpop), or the prologue to another (the New Rock Revolution). Now I'm hoping to prove this music, which formed an uneasy hinterland between cultures and centuries, was more than just a stopgap. *When Quiet Was the New Loud* includes sections on both the big-selling albums from the time (*The Man Who*; *Parachutes*; *White Ladder*), as well as others which arguably haven't fared so well in the public memory: Alfie's extended summer sigh *If You Happy With You Need Do Nothing*; The Electric Soft Parade's neo-psych beauty *Holes in the Wall*; and Lowgold's stately debut *Just Backward of Square*, among others. I'll also take in a couple of diversions, though never straying too far from the gentle road: Mull Historical Society's *Loss* and Snow Patrol's *When It's All Over We Still Have To Clear Up*, while not necessarily considered records central to the era, were

---

[7] This was arranged and endorsed by several other senior members of staff – come on, I wasn't *that* confident.

nevertheless in the mix, and more than merit a re-listen. In fact, the nebulous parameters of the New Acoustic Movement – along with its unfashionable reputation – meant that few mentioned here actually identified as part of it. Yet *something* undeniably connects them. Over five chapters – the demise of Britpop; the rise of a new, introspective Manchester wave; the stratospheric success of Coldplay and Snow Patrol; the 'New Acoustic Movement'; and the bands who pointed the way ahead – this book is an attempt to find out what that something is.

When I told friends I was writing about the New Acoustic Movement, they reacted with incredulity: 'Why on earth would you want to do *that*?!' was a typical response. The short answer is: I was there. I bought and loved these records. And though they'll deny it up and down, so did my peers. If you dig into those outraged responses, you'll find they come from a place of grudging, secret affection; many who now dismiss this music's impact also acknowledge a long-suppressed, clandestine purchase of *Parachutes* or *The Man Who*.

But what's the point in feeling shameful? A healthy way to think of these albums is like old schoolmates: we may not have much in common with them now, but they were there at a formative time for us – and that's often where the strongest, most enduring relationships are forged. So if the bond is that strong, why haven't these bands stuck around in our collective consciousness to the same extent as their nineties or noughties peers? Were they unlucky to be sandwiched between louder musical movements? Or was it their initially indifferent approach to fashion and politics – factors which need to coalesce to create a truly vibrant cultural 'moment' like Britpop? Perhaps it was something as banal as the lack of a snappy name: no one quite knew what to call this period, and it remains nameless today. And there is a final, awkward truth about where many physical copies of these albums ended up: they were sadly destined to leave a conspicuous trace in second-hand stores and charity shops. Because, with the dawning of a new technological era, the CD boom was coming to an end – and the public were ready to digitise.

As it turned out, 2001 represented the peak of the CD epoch, with downloads poised to overtake and then dominate musical consumption. In his spirited defence of the format for *The Quietus*, James Toth describes the CD's 'precipitous fall: Since peak plastic in 2001, CD sales have dropped 88%, from 712 million units to 85.4 million in 2017, according to Nielsen Music.' While that's a staggering statistic, it's also amazing to think that until very recently, bands were still not only releasing CD singles, but releasing *two versions* of them. It was a model that simply couldn't last, and the acoustic movement was set to bear the brunt of the changes. David Bowie, ever the game-changer, was the first major-label artist to release a downloadable album, *Hours*, in 1999. Since then, downloading has become the norm – and after weathering the digital storm for a decade or so, vinyl has also seen a huge recent increase in sales. As a result, CD uptake was eroded from both sides: reviled equally by LP purists after an authentic crackle, and by MP3 enthusiasts looking for portable audio perfection. The cluster of bands covered in this book were among the last of the big CD sellers; to be associated with a format that had rapidly become disposable looked fatal for their own longevity.

This book is a celebration, but it isn't revisionism. I know too well where a lot of these acts stand in people's minds and I know that, for many, the years covered in this book represent a period of musical stagnation. I'm inclined to disagree: there is gold to be found on every album here, and revisiting them has been both joyful and revealing. With this book, I want to make a case for the uncool. I also want to provide you with a playful and generous view of an era which, although it happened so recently, is already being purposefully forgotten.

In our current turbulent climate, where so much of life is loud and cruel, there is a lot to be said for a more measured approach. Humility, compassion and patience aren't words associated much with our culture or politics anymore, so perhaps the time has come for a bit of reflection. I invite you to sit with this (mostly) quiet music for a few hours, and rediscover its pleasures. But more than anything, I hope this book performs the function for which it is mainly written: to prompt affectionate memories of a time when all that was murky and melancholic stood at the vanguard of popular music – when the meek, however briefly, really did inherit the earth.

A note on selection, and a disclaimer

I haven't set out to write an exhaustive history of the acoustic era, this is simply a way of looking at the recent past afresh, and to try to make sense of an era that often felt ill-defined. The subtitle refers to celebration, and I've tried to keep it that way; so many of these artists took a critical kicking over the years that it seems pointless to dish out another one. Not that I would want to.

As this is partly a personal book, I've featured albums that struck a note with me at the time, or that I felt deserved critical reappraisal. Needless to say, there are many records from the time that I'd love to write about in future – and I've uncovered a whole lot more in the process of putting the book together. Your favourite might not have made it in, and I apologise if that's the case. But enough caveats: let's get started.

1. Staying in for the Summer:

The Chill of Britpop, and a New Beginning

Travis – *The Man Who*
David Gray – *White Ladder*
Dido – *No Angel*

I was too late for Britpop. *Parklife* and *Different Class* came out before I was ten years old. 'Roll With It' versus 'Country House' went over my head as simply 'something on the news' – only as interesting as Cantona's kung-fu kick, or Pierce Brosnan as James Bond, or someone called Martin Bashir interviewing someone called Princess Diana. At that age, I was concerned with more important things: what Dennis the Menace would get up to next week; where my next packet of super sour Nerds was coming from; mastering rock-the-cradle on my Fireball yo-yo. By the time music became a serious preoccupation, I was only hearing the darker echoes of Britpop. One of my tentative early purchases was Blur's self-titled album, about a year after its release (on cassette, from Woolworths, naturally). As the final track 'Essex Dogs' grumbled into the distance, I remember being intrigued but not amazed: that appreciation would only come later, when I could place *Blur* in the context of the band's other work. Even then, I was conscious of arriving at a shindig where the hosts were already tidying up the empty bottles.

By the end of 1998, the optimism of Blair and Britpop sat unreachably on the other side of a chasm created by two chastening, nation-altering events: Princess Diana's death in August 1997, and the subsequent period of unprecedented mass grief; and the following year, the England football team's ignominious exit from the 1998 World Cup in France, during which a red card for David Beckham turned him overnight from 'Goldenballs' into a figure of cruelly unjustified hatred. The goodwill that had swept Tony Blair to power the previous year was also rapidly diminishing. Things had failed to 'get better', with many beginning to feel New Labour was not so very different from Old Tory after all. On 14th March, *NME* published a cover which captured the national mood. It featured a picture of Blair and a simple, devastating question: 'Ever Had the Feeling You've Been Cheated?'

Britpop's previously reliable twin engines were beginning to stutter by this point, too. Blur were ravaged by infighting, overindulgence and the agonising disintegration of Damon Albarn's long-term relationship with Elastica frontwoman Justine Frischmann. The resulting music on their 1999 album *13*, while frequently astonishing, confirmed there would be no return to the chipper, park-bothering personas of just a few years earlier. Oasis were bedevilled by similar rifts, as the simmering tension between Liam and Noel Gallagher repeatedly threatened to boil over in 1997 and '98 during their promotional duties for *Be Here Now*. The two bands who had represented so much about Britain in the nineties were now becoming detached from their own cultural 'moment' – and consumer confidence began to erode as a result. In his excellent memoir, *Going Deaf for a Living*, Steve Lamacq sums up the feeling at the time, remembering 1998 and 1999 as 'lean years for music … The money that swirled around during the Britpop era was starting to ebb away and the industry was slow to react.' That sluggishness, that sudden loss of identity, was also reflected in the rapid rise of an insurgent American genre: rap metal. Fred Durst and Limp Bizkit were set to dominate the UK charts, with second and third albums *Significant Other* (1999) and *Chocolate Starfish and the Hot Dog Flavored Water* (2000) posting enormous sales both here and worldwide. By the turn of the millennium, Durst and his band were one of the hottest musical properties on the planet, selling 400,000 copies of *Chocolate Starfish* on the first day of its release in the US. 'Take A Look Around's appearance on the hotly-anticipated *Mission Impossible* sequel *M:i-2* (2000) raised the band's profile even further. The millennium year represented the genre's peak: Linkin Park's *Hybrid Theory* and Papa Roach's *Infest*, also released in 2000, both experienced mainstream adoration, crowding the charts with their hyper-masculine imagery and brash, uncompromising lyrics. Hardly surprising, then, that there was also a growing appetite for another, gentler kind of music. Things were changing fast, yet as the idols of the nineties began to slide sorrowfully away, there was one band who convincingly straddled the two eras, for a while at least: Travis.

★★★

'A year ago today we played over at the Other Stage. It was a beautiful, sunny day, and everyone was giving it "wahey, sun! Brilliant!" and I was there going, "I can see a big cloud coming," and no one believed me… until we played this song.' And then they play it.

Having spent many formative moments in the shadow of the Pyramid Stage, I know a full field when I see one. And watching back the video footage of Travis' Saturday headline slot at the 2000 edition of Glastonbury Festival – which I was a fraction too young to attend – I see the natural arena at the heart of Worthy Farm is *packed*. Tens of thousands of revellers have convened to see a young Scottish band who, the previous year, scooped two Brit awards and secured their first number one with their second album, *The Man Who*. As if to indicate just how rapidly their star was rising, Travis took to the stage *after* Pet Shop Boys. In an interview with *Music Week* in 2017, Healy recalls thinking 'Why are we going on after them? They're fucking massive!' Yet Travis were, suddenly, massive themselves: their fellow headliners that year were The Chemical Brothers, at the height of their powers and reportedly on coruscating form; and one David Bowie. In a 2018 list, *The Telegraph* ranked Glastonbury 2000 as the seventh best of all time. While that high placing may largely have been due to the Thin White Duke's presence, Travis more than played their part: 'Why Does It Always Rain On Me?' certainly sparked a singalong to match the festival's biggest.

As he nears the end of their signature hit, Healy takes what appears to be a risk – even though he knows, deep down, that everything is alright. He strums the opening notes of the final verse, and then he steps away from the microphone, tilts his head towards the crowd, and cups his hand to his ear, inviting the crowd to sing his song for him. They oblige – and how. Everything about Travis' performance that night suggests a band in what Neil Tennant, when describing his own band's purple patch, called the 'imperial phase': brimming with the confidence of an outfit in full control of their material and their audience. As 'Why Does It Always Rain On Me?' draws to a close, Healy cannot resist an enormous grin and a raised fist. Where did it all go right?

Three quarters of what would become Travis – Healy, drummer Neil Primrose and guitarist Andy Dunlop – began their musical lives in the early nineties, first meeting in 1991 while studying at the Glasgow School of Art. Andy cut his teeth in a cabaret band named Running Red, which originally featured a female vocalist, Catherine Maxwell. Neil soon joined the lineup as the band's drummer, and they altered their style (to Jefferson Starship-esque MOR), as well as their name, to the *White Album*-inspired Glass Onion.

Fran, meanwhile, was dissatisfied with the paintings he was producing at college, ditching his degree altogether – by 1993 he was making ends meet through retail work in Glasgow, while his friends graduated. But having realised he was first and foremost a singer-songwriter, he was by now seeking musical comrades. Although Glass Onion's musical stylings were not necessarily to Fran's taste, their chops were undeniable; he approached them and asked to join. It was to be the beginning of an extraordinary career. Maxwell exited the lineup and Healy took over primary vocal and songwriting duties, striving to push the band in a more professional direction. They quickly gained a fervent following in the city, and became a regular fixture at student nights, prevailing despite Healy's later assertions that Glass Onion were 'shit on a digestive'. Knowing he was capable of more, he signed on the dole and took off to Millport, a holiday resort on the island of Cumbrae, 'with the sole intention of writing the best song I'd ever written'. He came pretty close – returning with the raucously anthemic 'All I Want To Do Is Rock'.

With financial help from Fran's mum, the band then recorded a demo tape, *The Glass Onion EP*, and sent a copy out to record companies. It was evidently well-received; following a chaotic showcase at the Stones Bar in Edinburgh in October 1995, the band agreed to a publishing deal with Sony Music. This development prompted a personnel reshuffle which saw the departure of Glass Onion's original bassist and keyboardist, the brothers Chris and Geoff Martyn, as the band headed further towards their more rock-oriented sound. They also changed their name – a nod to Harry Dean Stanton's character Travis Henderson from the movie *Paris, Texas*. From there, things began to move. Their college friend Dougie Payne was persuaded to join as the new bassist – despite not actually being able to play bass at the time.[8] With the lineup settled, Healy and co. started rehearsing the material for the band's first full-length, with 'All I Want To Do Is Rock' forming the centrepiece. The Sony publishing deal had focused the minds of the band, but they remained unsigned. In a bid to secure label representation and increase their visibility, they relocated to London, pitching up together in a house in Haringey. They spent much of 1996 in the rehearsal studio, playing small gigs when they came along (including The Dublin Castle in Camden), honing their stagecraft and writing new material. After being talked down from another new band name, Red Telephone Box, the band settled on it for their own label, on which they released a limited pressing of 'All I Want To Do Is Rock'.[9] It was promptly

[8] He was reportedly given a two-week crash course, playing along to a cassette of the band's demos.
[9] Red Telephone Box was resurrected in 2008 for the release of the band's sixth album, *Ode to J. Smith* – they have used it for all subsequent releases.

named *Melody Maker*'s single of the week – a development which hinted at just how far things were about to progress.

The next few months saw Travis realise several dreams in quick succession. First, they signed a record deal with Andy Macdonald, who at the time was with Go! Discs, but snapped up the band for his new imprint, Independiente. They were scheduled to record their album in December – but not before fulfilling an unexpected publicity coup. The buzz surrounding the band had clearly reached high places: Travis made their national TV debut, appearing on *Later... with Jools Holland* at the beginning of that month, still with just one single under their belts. Their fellow performers that day were Sting, Tricky and Lionel Richie. Buoyed by a solid performance, a cluster of potential hits and a growing reputation, the band turned their attention to recording their first LP, *Good Feeling*. In an unlikely turn of events, they recorded it over the Atlantic, in Woodstock – a decision that seems to have been purely logistical due to a lack of space in London. Legendary producer Steve Lillywhite hosted them at the remote Bearsville Studios, in what would prove an enormously fruitful and efficient session – the album was recorded in just four days, with the band playing 'as live' for the most part. With recording wrapped, Healy decided to close out the year by taking a solo holiday to Eilat, Israel, to wind down and perhaps write a song or two. Luckily for him, the weather was awful.

Travis toured relentlessly through 1997, with *Good Feeling* released that September. It was an appropriately boisterous collection, indebted to classic rock – a faithfully rendered portrait of an energetic and hungry young band. Much like other tentative debuts from established rock bands – Blur's *Leisure* or Radiohead's *Pablo Honey*, for example – there were only hints of the direction they were ultimately heading in. The ballad 'More Than Us' provided the best indication. Bedecked with warm, inviting strings and a noticeably more robust structure, it stood out as a vehicle for Healy's rapidly maturing voice (the more grizzled vocal stylings that pepper *Good Feeling* would virtually disappear from his palette by *The Man Who*). Although *Good Feeling* was received well by critics and breached the Top Ten, it quickly slid down the charts, leaving Healy disappointed.

'I'm beginning to realise that luck is the most important thing,' he lamented. Fortunately, they were about to embark on the biggest shows of their career.

Earlier that year, at a 100 Club gig headlined by Travis – and one which would effectively define their next steps – Noel Gallagher, Jonny Greenwood and producer Nigel Godrich were all in attendance. Noel was so impressed by what he saw that night that he asked Travis to support Oasis on their *Be Here Now* tour, which incorporated several massive UK shows at the tail end of 1997, and the West Coast leg of their American dates in early 1998 (Cornershop played the East Coast). It was an invitation that, for a band desperate to raise their profile, represented a golden ticket. As it transpired, the shows became infamous for their sprawling, indulgent nature – they even featured props from the cover of *Be Here Now*, including a Rolls Royce and a red telephone box which were wheeled onstage at certain cues. 'It was like supporting The Rolling Stones, they were so big back then,' Healy remembers. Yet Oasis were kind and encouraging to Travis – perhaps they spotted something of themselves in the young Scots. According to Healy, Liam was once brought to tears by a backstage rendition of 'Luv'; Noel would sometimes join the band on stage for 'All I Want To Do Is Rock'. For a young band learning from, and hoping to emulate, Oasis' achievements, it proved an eye-opening introduction to the higher echelons of rock'n'roll superstardom. They were soon to make that ascent themselves.

The band then headed to France, where they spent three weeks recording with producer Mike Hedges in Normandy. The sessions were positive but Healy was dissatisfied with his own writing efforts. The band returned to the UK for a rethink and selected Nigel Godrich as producer for the next set of sessions. These were more fruitful, and the resulting patchwork – having worked with two producers and in a total of six studios – formed the eleven songs on *The Man Who*.[10] As Dougie Payne, comparing the album to *Good Feeling*, said at the time, 'We've recorded it over six months in six different studios, using more instrumentation, and it's turned into this weirdly cohesive piece of work.' He was not wrong.

[10] The title is partly lifted from Oliver Sacks's classic work of popular psychology, *The Man Who Mistook His Wife for a Hat*.

The gulf between *Good Feeling* and *The Man Who* is enormous when the two records are considered back-to-back, and the change in pace, while masterful in retrospect, was a huge risk. It put the band firmly in more serious, 'adult rock' territory – Healy's description of the upcoming second record as 'an album for staying in rather than going out' can only have been met with a guarded reception from both critics and fans primed for further bounciness. The release of 'Writing to Reach You' in March 1999 confirmed the arrival of this more mature outlook, as did the restrained artwork: a desolate field underneath a grey sky, with a silver weather balloon the only object to draw the eye. Where Britpop's colour scheme had been glossy, garish and urban, Travis and their contemporaries now stripped back their visuals to a more muted palette, often depicting natural spaces.[11] As *The Man Who* approached and more songs were released, the masses were evidently won over by the band's new careworn direction, and Travis began to bother the serious end of the charts for the first time. 'Driftwood', released that May, was a gorgeous paean to rootlessness, and debuted at number 13, their highest chart position to date – a promising sign ahead of the album's arrival the following week.

The Man Who was far from the accessible pop-rock record its enormous successes might now suggest. Relistens reveal it to be darker and more complex than many gave it credit for at the time, representing a huge step forward for the band in terms of both sound and songcraft. 'Writing to Reach You' and 'Driftwood' had hinted at the quality within; the enormous chorus of 'Turn' and the delicacy of 'The Last Laugh of the Laughter' confirmed this was a band now capable of considerable range. But it was the track immediately after 'Turn', 'Why Does It Always Rain On Me?', written by Healy during his washout holiday in Israel (chorus), and a hotel room in Madrid (verses and bridge), that stood apart. Speaking to *Songwriting* magazine in 2019, Healy reveals his trepidation at the departure in sound: 'It was very quiet and subdued, and completely in opposition to everything that was happening in the charts and on the radio at the time. So I think we all thought we were doomed.' As it turned out, that 'opposition' was exactly what the public were looking for.

[11] See also: Chris Martin trudging over a drizzly beach at dawn in the video for 'Yellow', or Kings of Convenience huddled beside a Bergen lake on the cover of *Quiet is the New Loud*.

Elsewhere on *The Man Who,* the mood darkens further. Godrich had only recently wrapped on Radiohead's *OK Computer,* and that record's influence is traceable on tracks like 'The Fear', with its 'Karma Police'-like outro, and on 'Luv's airless, ghostly atmosphere. For Dougie, the former encapsulated the band's newfound message: 'If there's an underlying theme to this album, it's that you shouldn't be afraid to be vulnerable.' He may as well have been talking about the music that defined the next five years. Regret and inadequacy return again and again as themes: 'Ever since I was young / I had no choice' laments Healy on 'As You Are', an account of being 'led on' – and, presumably, not feeling able to act upon such invitations. It was about as far from 'Rock'n'Roll Star's bombastic certitude as it was possible to get – and mournful closer 'Slide Show' presented another defining break with the past. Its references to nineties hits, scattered through the chorus – 'A Design for Life', 'Devil's Haircut' and 'Wonderwall' (again) – all flash by in the protagonist's head. It's a sad, quiet montage, a stately summation of the past decade. 'Slow down, slow down', it implores. The nineties were doing just that.

Yet there is a sting in the tail. Let the CD run on after 'Slide Show' fades out, past the sound of a car door slamming, and you find raucous hidden track 'Blue Flashing Light' – a song more befitting of Glass Onion than the company it keeps here. It's a slightly bizarre inclusion, but also serves as a useful reference point: a reminder to new fans of where the band had come from. On *The Man Who* there was no doubt where they were going.

Healy's soaring voice was the star of the album this time around – and critics rightly hailed it as such. *Pitchfork*'s review was especially complimentary: 'Some of [Healy's] notes will make your cheeks tingle … on *The Man Who,* power comes from restraint and space.' Tellingly, that review also speaks of a weariness with the Britpop schtick, which is dismissed as a 'cognizant conceit … the raw humility of Travis is refreshing'. However, the praise was not quite universal: the *NME* were more sceptical in their 6/10 review, with Stuart Bailie lamenting the loss of the band's lighter side: 'Back then [the *Good Feeling* era], Travis could plug into what they called "the stupid factor" and boogie along with a saving hint of irony. We miss all that, actually.' The reviews were a good example of the coverage that would describe much of the acoustic movement: initially reluctant praise overwhelmed by the weight of public goodwill.

In the end, the critical response turned out not to matter, and *The Man Who* became the first classic album of the post-Britpop era. It entered the charts at number 5 in May 1999 and, thanks to the ubiquity of 'Why Does It Always Rain On Me?' during the summer festival season, continued to bother the Top Ten throughout the summer. The band's set on Glastonbury's Other Stage (a year before their step up to the Pyramid) was marked, memorably, by a freak deluge as they began playing the song. It's a moment which has since become part of rock folklore, yet at the time the band were unhappy with their showing – and with the weather. As Healy recalls, 'We all thought it was a really below-par performance and a literal washout. When I got home that night, I switched the TV on and the presenters on the Glastonbury highlights were hailing us as the performance of the festival.' The set was a phenomenon, generating national news coverage and effectively turning Travis into household names overnight. Music festivals were by now big business: having been televised since 1994, and undergone huge commercialisation throughout the nineties, a well-timed appearance at Glastonbury could rapidly shape a band's fortune. By the time they took to the stage just a few weeks later at V Festival on Sunday 22nd August, *The Man Who* had been announced as that week's number one album.[12] It would spend nine weeks there, then a further two years in the Top 100 – reportedly one in twenty houses in the UK owned a copy at one stage. It was the third best-selling album of 1999 and, incredibly, the fourteenth best-selling album of 2000. At the time of writing it is number 43 in the all-time UK best-seller list. Travis had accidentally ushered in a different breed of guitar music – one that, although closely related to Britpop, was just distinctive enough to feel new.

One of the key differences between Travis and the Britpop set was a comparative lack of machismo. But they were keen to stand apart from the prevailing culture of the late nineties in other ways, too. Perhaps mindful of the political knots that many Britpop bands had tied themselves up in the latter half of the decade, Travis elected

---

[12] Travis played the *NME* Stage at V that year, part of a madly eclectic bill that also featured experimental oddities dEUS, Super Furry Animals, and headliner James Brown.

to keep schtum on their leanings, at least to begin with; many of their contemporaries would choose to do the same. In a *Spin* profile of the band in 2001 pointing out that 'Travis and Coldplay seem to distinguish themselves by shying away from the twilight idealism of their elders', Healy responds to a comment from Damon Albarn that the new batch of bands are 'boring and apolitical' with a statement that largely sums up the initial stance of the acoustic set: 'Blur wore their politics on their sleeves. Going even further back, U2 wore theirs like a massive overcoat. Well, we carry ours in our wallets.' Healy's activist side would lay dormant as his band continued their rise, before the cataclysmic events of the post-millennium years significantly altered his worldview.

The Man Who was the commercial pinnacle for Travis, but that didn't preclude further brilliance. They then released my personal favourite single 'Coming Around' as a stand-alone between albums; it reached number five in the charts. Like *The Man Who,* 2001's follow-up *The Invisible Band* – this time recorded in Los Angeles, again with Godrich at the helm – also reached the number one spot. Although it too had fraught origins – Healy remembers 'nothing was gelling' in a *Billboard* interview from 2001 – the band eventually hit their groove, 'banging out tunes like the four mates we've always been'. The collection would spawn three Top Twenty singles, including 'Sing', which continued the band's penchant for single-word titles, and the blissful 'Flowers in the Window', written in Normandy during the first sessions for *The Man Who. The Invisible Band* contains many immaculate pieces of songwriting: the penultimate track 'Indefinitely' might even stake a convincing claim as the band's best four minutes. The album closes with 'The Humpty Dumpty Love Song'[13] which, despite its nursery rhyme reference, was probably the most sophisticated arrangement Travis had attempted to date; a swelling, multi-layered story-song that closes with a chilling sustained orchestral note. With each album, Travis were maturing, asking bolder questions of themselves and their capabilities.

Two well-documented events shaped the direction they would take next. The first was 9/11 and the subsequent 'War on Terror', a

---

[13] Perhaps a knowing reference to Fran's star turn as an egg with legs in the video for 'Coming Around'.

global unravelling which seemed to disturb and politically galvanise the band in equal measure. Even as recently as 2016, Healy refers to it as a pivotal moment: 'I haemorrhaged confidence in the political system during Iraq. Millions of people marched and we couldn't make any difference.' The second event took place closer to home: a serious injury to Neil Primrose in July 2002, who fractured three vertebrae in a swimming pool accident, prompting Travis to cancel much of their planned touring around *The Invisible Band*. While Neil entered a prolonged and painful recovery period, the band took stock. 'The enforced hiatus gave us a perspective on what had happened before and what had to happen next,' says Dougie in an *Independent* interview in 2003. It was to signal another musical reinvention – one that reflected their increasing disillusion. Healy put it in the starkest terms: 'I have had the feeling for the past few weeks, ever since the war started, that it's not really my world anymore. I think a lot of people feel that.' Coming from a place of such personal and societal anxiety, third album *12 Memories* (2003) was inevitably weighed down with big questions. The album's opening trio of songs announced a very different Travis: the claustrophobic 'Quicksand'; 'The Beautiful Occupation', which bluntly alluded to the invasion of Iraq; and lead single 'Re-Offender', an unflinching depiction of domestic abuse. 'Peace the Fuck Out', their most overtly political song, further confirmed that the band were unconcerned with making something pretty or consolatory this time around: they were pissed off, and you could hear it. And while proceedings mellowed somewhat on the album's second half, their newfound ambition was unmistakable – final track 'Walking Down the Hill's minimal piano and skittering percussion recalled no artist more clearly than Radiohead. *12 Memories* was a million miles away from *Good Feeling* and 'Tied to the '90s' – because Travis no longer were.

Yet the making of *12 Memories*, and a lukewarm reaction from the press to their new direction, seemed to exhaust the group; a long hiatus ensued. Coldplay's debut album *Parachutes*, released between *The Man Who* and *The Invisible Band*, appeared to further shift popular focus away from the Scots. The two bands' rise to fame during 1999 and 2000 consolidated the feeling that music was entering a new era, and for many the two are inextricably linked. And while it's true

Travis and Coldplay share some sonic ground, they often diverge more than they match – Healy himself says he 'could not think of two more different approaches to art' when comparing them.[14] In a BBC Radio Scotland documentary celebrating *The Man Who*'s 20th anniversary, he reflects on his band's brief time at the very top of the musical mountain, and Coldplay's continued presence there:

> There is no one up there and it is quite barren and lonely. But Chris [Martin] is still up there. He's up there playing tennis with Bono … But you have got to ask yourself, why would anyone want to remain at the top of Mount Everest where there is no one to talk to? You can't really write from the heart up there. You need to be on the ground.

Healy and his band of friends had shown the ambition to scale the heights, and the maturity to realise fame was not for them. They decided to come back down to earth, but the band's impact on the nation is still evident today. Not least because whenever the heavens open, someone, somewhere, will be singing *that song*. It will always rain on us – and we'll always have Travis to provide the soundtrack.

★★★

[14] Chris Martin has always held Travis in high regard – once describing himself as a 'poor man's Fran Healy'.

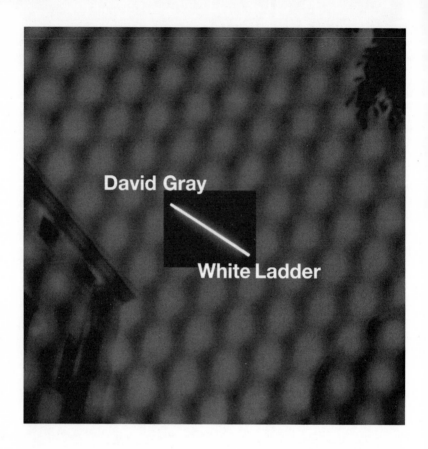

1998 was a pivotal year for another artist unknowingly on the verge of their greatest success: David Gray, who quietly released his fourth album, *White Ladder*, on a limited run on his own label that November.

Gray was born into an affluent middle-class family in Sale, Greater Manchester in 1968. The family relocated to the tiny coastal village of Solva, in rural Pembrokeshire, when David was nine. From a young age, he was fascinated by his parents' record collection, which extensively featured Van Morrison and Bob Dylan – singers who would become his primary musical influences. Morrison's *Astral Weeks* was, and remains, a totemic collection for Gray: 'I can think of no greater moment of inspiration in popular music history … From start to finish, there's no other record like it.' He began writing songs in his early teens on an old guitar which was lying around the house – but it would take a while for the Dylan / Morrison influence to manifest. He formed a band with three school friends, The Prawns (later The Vacuums) who would perform at school discos, channelling myriad forms of rock'n'roll as best they could: Jimi Hendrix, The Who, The Cramps and The Cure were all apparently in the mix. This chaotic blend of influences, while undoubtedly fun to play, reportedly did not endear them to the Pembrokeshire scene, and The Vacuums fizzled out once school wound up for the boys.

Just like the members of Travis, Gray then took the art school route, first attending college in Carmarthen, then moving up to Liverpool to study at the College of Art. Gray was a skilled painter – reportedly making £2000 one summer from the sale of his early work – and he also played in a series of college bands, including the incongruously-named Waiting For Deffo, with whom he would end up recording a demo tape. The band sent their effort off without much hope of a response, but it eventually fell into the hands of an A&R man at Polydor, Rob Holden, who was to play a pivotal role in Gray's life. Holden was impressed by what he heard of WFD – and especially with Gray's voice. He travelled to Liverpool to see the band and, having evidently identified Gray as the core talent, offered to manage him; Waiting For Deffo disbanded. Holden promptly quit Polydor and added Gray to his fledgling management roster,[15] eventually helping him to secure a deal with Hut Records.[16] It was the beginning of an erratic, bamboozling and ultimately rewarding career in music.

Gray's three pre-*White Ladder* albums, while critically lauded and adored by a cult following, only hinted at the astonishing heights that lay in store. Hut released the brooding *A Century Ends* (1993), and the inconsistent *Flesh* (1994) – the latter reportedly Gray's least favourite album. Both records failed to shift copies in any great number, and there was already a sense that Gray was a man out of time – with baggy and rave now at their peak, the public appetite for

[15] Which also included Phil and Paul Hartnoll, who were by now on the precipice of fame as Orbital. Gray's relationship with the brothers would soon become familial: he married Olivia Hartnoll in 1993.
[16] The label already boasted The Verve and The Auteurs on their books at this point, and would find continued success later in the nineties with Gomez, most notably their Mercury Prize-winning debut *Bring It On* (1998), and *Liquid Skin* (1999).

a Van Morrison-like voice was virtually non-existent. Furthermore, the critical response to both records, which saddled Gray with the 'new Bob Dylan' tag (optimistically lobbed towards so many earnest singer-songwriter types in the nineties), cannot have helped matters.[17] As Dave Anderson, who produced *A Century Ends*, also reflected: 'I don't think the label knew what to do with it, to be honest. At that time, singer-songwriters were as unfashionable as they could possibly be and I don't think they knew how to promote it – so they didn't!' Hut didn't even release a single from *Flesh*; Gray recalls 'a few posters went up and then they dropped me'. Despite these hurdles, there was no denying Gray's early output contained a foreshadowing of his later brilliance. 'Shine', the opening track on *A Century Ends* – and an eventual hit in Ireland, the country where he would find his most receptive audience – is a strong example, showcasing Gray's imperious voice and his penchant for the anthemic. *PopMatters* sum up the general feeling in their retrospective review of his early releases: 'The work found on *A Century Ends*, *Flesh*, and *The EPs 92-94* shouldn't be seen as a mark on Gray's career; rather they should be taken as a stark reminder of the monumental climb that he had to undertake before he could finally take a breather.'

Gray was released from Hut after *Flesh*, only to be picked up by EMI America almost immediately. He had toured the US with Shawn Colvin around the time of her 1992 album, *Fat City* – as well as with Maria McKee and Kirsty MacColl – and had evidently won fans in high places across the pond. Dissatisfied with the public response to his first two albums, Gray was only too ready to switch it up at the behest of his new employers, piling on the guitars for *Sell, Sell, Sell*. But the shift in style proved difficult to nail down: a tortuous recording process saw Gray and his band piecing the record together in studios on both sides of the Atlantic, leaving a long list of collaborators in their wake. Despite its protracted delivery, *Sell, Sell, Sell* was Gray's poppiest and most accessible effort to date. Unfortunately, EMI had the same problems as Hut: ironically, they didn't know how to sell him. The American wing of the label was also hitting troubled financial straits. Gray bought out his contract;

[17] Those Dylan comparisons dried up once the original hit form again later in the decade.

Warner ended their publishing contract with him, too. Now back in the UK, Gray found himself three albums in, but without a band or a label – and unlikely to find either unless his situation seriously improved. A complete rethink was required.

In a 2020 interview with Dave Simpson in *The Guardian*, Gray attributes his change of fortunes to a tentative embrace of club culture. 'I'd been going to Orbital gigs since the early nineties and wanted to try on clubbier culture and make music that expressed living at that moment.' Gray had parted ways with his band after *Sell, Sell, Sell* – apart from his long-time percussionist and collaborator, Clune.[18] Now working largely from Gray's bedroom in Stoke Newington, and with the help of a newly-acquired Roland Groovebox MC-303, the pair began to work through ideas for new songs, jamming regularly with their minimal setup of keyboard, computer and processed drum and bass. Gray recalls the breakthrough in the Simpson interview: 'I secreted myself away … during a dinner party and the chords and lyrics for "Please Forgive Me" fell out of the sky. The hairs on my neck stood on end.' It was a song that provided the catalyst for the rest of *White Ladder*. Gray and Clune hooked up with producer Iestyn Polson, whose input would also prove crucial to establishing the album's sound. Little did the trio realise they were producing a modern masterpiece.

Writing about *White Ladder* is not easy, because we now can't imagine life without it. It made the leap from novelty to normality in an extraordinarily short timeframe, achieving not only commercial success, but the kind of elevated resonance granted only to the most lasting cultural events. As a retrospective *Pitchfork* review has it: '[*White Ladder*] subsequently achieved the rarefied level of ubiquity where its omnipresence became one of its defining characteristics.' At two decades' remove, however, Gray's best album reveals itself as more nuanced, enjoyable and artistically coherent than its frequent hecklers might have you believe. It has become part of our national language, perhaps the only album in this book that has transcended its 'album-ness' entirely. Yet it is also a record that, despite its near-messianic ubiquity – both in the year 2000 and for many years afterwards – still contains its hidden corners.

---

[18] Craig McClune, known universally as Clune, was far more than simply Gray's drummer: he is credited as a co-writer on three of *White Ladder*'s ten tracks, and sings harmonies on 'Babylon'.

If you haven't listened to *White Ladder* for a while, electric surprises abound. 'Please Forgive Me' is still strikingly pretty: plaintive piano; elliptical guitar line; something approaching a breakbeat, so fittingly suggestive of that 'lightning running through my veins'. Then comes 'Babylon'. Given its eventual monopoly over the rest of his back catalogue, Gray is understandably reluctant to talk about his most popular song, although he revealed in a *Music Radar* interview in 2012 he 'hadn't really taken [it] seriously' until Polson's production fleshed it out. It leaps from the speakers, even now: still borne up by those swelling strings at that precisely engineered yet impossibly affecting moment; still adorned by those twinkling flourishes of guitar and sampler. And after the euphoria, the comedown: 'Nightblindness' – which was added to later versions of the album, having proved a popular B-side – is memorably downbeat, the refrain 'What we gonna do when the money runs out?' reflecting the real worries Gray was having at the time, having poured his soul into music for vanishingly little reward.

The structure of *White Ladder* – and remember, it was released into what was still a broadly pre-playlist world, in which album mechanics counted for a lot – is clever too. Three of its most accessible songs: 'This Year's Love', 'Sail Away', and a desolate cover of Soft Cell's 'Say Hello Wave Goodbye', are placed at the end – ramping up the emotional engagement after the comparative experiments of its middle sequence. 'This Year's Love' – used on *Dawson's Creek* to memorable effect – is perhaps the pick of the bunch. A piano ballad of rare skill and subtlety, its appeal is found in the contrast between Gray's lyrics, which speak of the dizzying effects of new love, and his restrained, almost subdued delivery – pleasure tempered with both weariness and wariness. It was unlike anything else on the album, or indeed like Gray had attempted before – a song closer in sound and scope to the rarefied torch songs of Elton John. How exciting it must have been to record these songs; to sing them for the first time. Those 'why-wha-why-whys' and 'whoah-oh's, that hang on the end of Gray's lines, vocal filigrees that were kryptonite to certain corners of the press, now sound like realisations of joy: *this* is what I've been working towards, *this* is what could make me. He was right. *White Ladder*'s rueful ruminations on a decade lived too fast, and with too many regrets, was about to strike a chord with other nineties survivors on a scale that defies belief even now.

Given the subsequent commercial triumph of *White Ladder*, it is easy to forget that it was subject to a false start. Limited to 5000 copies and released by Gray on his own label, iht, in November 1998, the album initially failed to chart. Fittingly, the dancefloor was responsible for its second wind: 'Please Forgive Me' was given a white-label remix courtesy of Phil Hartnoll, and proved a surprise hit with the Ibiza crowd in summer 1999. Gray then supported Robbie Williams at his enormous Dublin Slane Castle show on 28th August that year,[19] just a week after Travis had hit number one with *The Man Who*. Finally, he was in the right place at the right time. It was only then that *White Ladder* began to move in earnest, especially in Ireland, where Gray had already established a far keener fanbase than anywhere else.[20] The album was then picked up and rereleased by EastWest in the UK, and then by Dave Matthews in the USA, as the first album on his new ATO label in May 2000. Matthews was already an enormous star in the States, and was a close friend of Gray's, the latter having opened for the Dave Matthews Band in support of *Sell, Sell, Sell* a few years earlier. Matthews had been casting around for a strong statement with which to kick off the venture; *White Ladder* was the perfect fit. 'When we first heard *White Ladder* … we begged him to let us put it on ATO. It really is one of my favourite records of all time.' And although the EastWest incarnation only snuck into the UK charts at number 69, *White Ladder* then simply *stuck around*. It would remain in the Top 100 for an incredible 175 weeks, between May 2000 and March 2003. In a retrospective interview with the Official Charts site in 2016, Gray recalls his rudimentary distribution methods after the iht release: 'Rob Holden … his hall was completely full with CDs … I had to load up my Volkswagen Golf and take them to a freight airport to get them to Ireland for Christmas. My car was loaded with about

[19] Williams was at this point riding high on his James Bond-channelling second album *I've Been Expecting You* (1998). Lead single 'Millennium', which reached number one in September 1998, was a potent pre-2000 anthem, a blend of nostalgia (the musical cue from John Barry's *You Only Live Twice* score), terrace-worthy lyrics ('come and have a go if you think you're hard enough') and the buzzword of the moment – to winning effect.

[20] At one stage, it was estimated that one in every four households in Ireland owned a copy of *White Ladder*.

2,500 CDs; it was scraping along the ground!' Gray could not have realised how tiny a fraction of his eventual sales he was shovelling into the boot that day.

For an album that was bought in such tremendous volume, not many people stared directly into the heart of *White Ladder* or realised the last-chance-saloon context of its making. Most listeners basked in the glow of its soundtrack-friendly singles, heard bits of it second-hand from buskers, who gobbled up its beginner-friendly chords, or as the soundtrack to the aperitif of yet another dinner party. It was a record that was listened to lightly; popular because of its outward simplicity. Eventually it became a victim of its own prominence, the hits eclipsing its creator's back catalogue in a way that echoes other great exponents of mid-tempo acoustic meditations like Del Amitri or Crowded House. The album brought opprobrium from the hipper music press too, quickly becoming a byword for everything they didn't like about the acoustic movement – notwithstanding that the movement was a construction of that selfsame media. Some of the criticism of *White Ladder* looks harsh in retrospect. 'Gray's eyes-closed sincerity will doubtless soundtrack every "empathic" black-and-white building society ad until cockroaches rule the earth,' was among the milder comments *NME* wrote in their disdainful review. Yet the censure was to prove irrelevant. Driven by those five inescapable singles, 'Babylon', 'This Year's Love', 'Please Forgive Me', 'Sail Away' and 'Say Hello, Wave Goodbye', *White Ladder* rapidly became a staple of both radios and living rooms – eventually shifting almost three million copies in the UK alone. It wasn't just one of the biggest albums of 2001 and 2002: it was the fifth biggest-selling album of the *decade*, and remains the biggest selling album of all time in Ireland. It was an achievement Gray would only partially be able to recreate.

The *White Ladder* album artwork had shown us two David Grays: on page one of the CD booklet, the moody singer-songwriter in classic pose, eyes down, left hand hooked behind his head. And on the inside back page, Gray caught mid-leap, mouth hanging open in a laughing yelp, a blur of energy and mischief. We often get this sense of Gray's unusually kinetic movement. His live presence is jerky and unpredictable, made famous by a seemingly unconscious head wobble during his livelier numbers. But *White Ladder*'s extraordinary rise seemed to poleaxe a little of that vim, perhaps unsurprising now that Gray was dealing with a strange, new pressure: expectation. Recalling the immediate aftermath of the record's success for an interview with *Vinyl Me Please*, Gray admits struggling to recreate the creative spark:

> I think the whole thing is complex, because [*White Ladder*] was made in a very sort of unselfconscious way, and then you're suddenly thrown into a reverse situation where you've got to try and create something else. It's very hard to find that comfortable natural place where you make music. It was an overwhelming, tumultuous period where I sort of shrank back into my shell. I didn't relish the world of fame and success and it wasn't something that I thought had any merit on its own terms.

It meant that Gray's follow-up album *A New Day At Midnight* (2002), while admirably preceded by the radio single 'Dead in the Water', was a hesitant affair, propped up with finicky electronics that couldn't quite rescue it from an odd feeling of inertia. You suspect Gray's ubiquity had worn down the patience of some critics; the reaction to *A New Day At Midnight* was another mix of hearty admiration and mild scorn. Nevertheless, it hit the number one spot and stayed in the charts for just over a year – Gray again proving a master of the long game. It's notable that he has always very much been an album artist: 'Babylon' remains his only Top Five single, yet *White Ladder* is the second highest selling album in the 'solo male artist' category of the century so far. That consistency is reflected in his sound, too, although it led some to accuse *A New Day At Midnight* of simply being *White Ladder* part two. Yet Gray freely admits to occasional sonic shortcomings: 'I've been a slow learner; in the language of sound, I'm not naturally linguistic…' His honesty about his processes, and regarding the struggles of his early career, have always lent him an air of the everyman – a character the public were craving, sick of 'lads' by the end of the extrovert nineties. Perhaps conscious that he risked painting himself into an introspective corner, Gray then decided to send up his best-known performance tic in the video for the second single, and *A New Day*

At Midnight's most uplifting cut, 'Be Mine'. The clip features Gray strumming along in inimitable style, charming a half-empty pub (a knowing callback to his formative years, perhaps), who all seem to be rubbing their necks... before Gray quite literally loses his head. The pub's dog sets off with it in his jaws, it gets hoofed around on a football pitch, then ends up in a poor lady's bicycle basket before coming to rest in a stable, right under a horse's posterior. It was a silly and self-deprecating statement, and a neat reminder that none of this should be taken too seriously, as some of the acoustic bands undoubtedly were by this point.

But it was 2005's *Life in Slow Motion*, a sombre, atmospheric collection, that felt like Gray's most rounded work yet. Despite its icy front cover, it was 'The One I Love' that brought Gray his second Top Ten hit with its warm, open optimism. 'Ain't No Love' – perhaps a belated reply to 'This Year's Love' – is also among the highlights, marrying Gray's ever-maturing voice with delicate strings and piano. 'Some days I'm bursting at the seams / with all my half-remembered dreams' was again evocative of the two-sided Gray. Finally, this was the sound of an artist comfortable in his own skin again, creating freely and honing his best qualities for maximum emotional impact. He was beginning to deal with the pressure of public expectation, and ready once more to invent on his own terms.

While he would never repeat the seismic impact of *White Ladder*, its legacy as one of the most potent markers of pre-millennial culture – perhaps even the last great pop album of the 20th century – is undeniable. In an interview with the *Irish Post* to discuss 2014's *Mutineers*, Gray hints that he has made peace with the strange glare of success: 'I feel free of the shackles of the past – completely. And in a weird way, because of that, more connected to it. Success and what has happened to me always threatens to suck you back towards it, and when you're trying to move forward suddenly that feels like a threat. But I know that chapter of my life is over.'

★★★

The domination of Britpop in the mid-nineties, along with the introduction in 1994 of stricter laws around large outdoor gatherings and 'repetitive beats', prompted the dwindling of rave culture as a mass movement in the UK. However, dance music was far from dead by the end of the decade. On a commercial level, it even went through something of a purple patch, buoyed by homegrown 'Big Beat' DJs like Fatboy Slim, The Chemical Brothers and Basement Jaxx, and reinforced by enormous one-off singles from the rest of the world, like Stardust's 'Music Sounds Better With You' (1998) and Armand van Helden's 'U Don't Know Me' (1999). Long-established clubbing utopias like Ibiza and Ayia Napa retained and even improved their cache among the UK rave crowd. It was a late renaissance which saw the rise of an increasingly necessary trend among veteran club-goers: a splinter genre of ambient house known as 'chillout'. Because while the super-clubs undoubtedly still held an appeal for the old-school ravers, there was also a palpable sense that, as the nineties wore on, their focus was being drawn irrevocably from the warehouse to the dinner table; from white-labels to compilation CDs. The 'last party' was beginning to wind down.

Chillout interacted naturally with the acoustic era. Turin Brakes were originally marketed as part of it; Kings of Convenience roped in many of its leading exponents for their remix album, *Versus* (2001); and David Gray's readiness to experiment with club culture in his work brought huge success with *White Ladder*. In turn, acoustic music was readily adopted for remix purposes, meaning many unassuming acts found themselves recast as unlikely dancefloor fillers. This cross-pollination worked the other way, too: while artists like Zero 7, Morcheeba, Röyksopp and Goldfrapp are more strongly associated with dance and electronica, they also made frequent appearances on the myriad acoustic/chillout compilations that adorned the CD racks of tastefully-lit dining rooms in the late nineties and early 2000s. The rise of these parallel genres reflected the maturation of a generation ready to settle down – or perhaps hunker down – in the face of a new chapter of history. 'Chilling out' represented the same kind of retreat as the acoustic movement did: by doing so, it was possible to stave off the anxieties of both future and past for just a little longer. The singer whom many saw as the encapsulation of this pre-millennial hesitancy, a feeling of 'safeness' – at least, in terms of her music – was Dido. But beneath her songs, which appealed to both acoustic and chillout fans, there lay an artist as driven as any of her Britpop predecessors.

Although she eventually became one of the biggest-selling album artists of the period covered in this book – and, indeed, of all time – Dido Florian Cloud de Bounevialle O'Malley Armstrong's route to stardom could hardly have been less conventional. Yet much like David Gray and *White Ladder*, it's now hard to imagine a musical map of the late nineties and early noughties in which Dido doesn't feature. *No Angel*, her 1999 debut, and its follow-up, *Life For Rent* (2003), rank among the top ten best-selling albums of the noughties – and her work left an indelible mark on the films, television shows, bedrooms and coffee shops of the beginning of the century. It is highly likely her talents would have eventually brought her success under any circumstances,[21] but her career was undeniably given a huge early push – first in America, then worldwide – from the unlikeliest of sources: Eminem. Before we get to Marshall Mathers, though, it's worth detailing Dido's early career, which is often overlooked in favour of her baseball-capped benefactor.

The younger sister of Faithless member Rollo Armstrong, the classically-named Dido was born on Christmas Day in 1971 (she has an 'official' birthday on 25th June), and grew up in Islington in a well-to-do but unusually quiet environment, with her publisher father and poet mother. As the family didn't own a TV or allow visitors, the young Dido was forced to make her own entertainment: she first learned recorder on an instrument 'appropriated' from school, and then moved on to other instruments including piano and guitar – allowing her to spend weekends away from the house at the Guildhall College of Music. As she grew older and felt increasingly stifled by her home life, Dido became more wayward. As a teenager she found a release in club culture and, having fallen out with her parents, left the family home and moved in with friends in a shared house. Then, in a move that speaks to her driven personality, she took a job at a literary agency and studied law on the side, reading up in particular about the music industry – the place she still had her heart set on.

By this point, Rollo was beginning studio sessions with Faithless as the band prepared their debut album, *Reverence* (1996). Dido inveigled her way into the setup, singing back-up vocals on a number of their early tracks (her contribution to 'Flowerstand Man' can be heard on *Reverence*; she also puts her recorder skills to good use on 'Angeline'). Her brother was initially reluctant to share the spotlight, as he recalled in a profile of the pair in May 2001. 'I'd been really lucky and my feeling was that it doesn't strike the same place twice. And maybe deep down I didn't want the competition. But she was absolutely determined, and when my sister's determined, that's it. It didn't matter what I said. She just went off on her own and found people to work with.' Dido had also by now written many of the songs that would go on to feature on *No Angel*, and she set about recording and sending out demos. These caught the ear of Arista

---

[21] *No Angel* had already sold hundreds of thousands of copies in the US before 'Stan' was released.

Records, who clearly saw the hit-making potential within, and offered her an enormous deal. She turned it down and signed with her brother's label, Cheeky.[22]

Then came two life-changing breaks. Firstly, 'Here With Me' was selected as the theme to Jason Katims's popular sci-fi high school drama *Roswell*, which ran for three series between 1999 and 2002. Then, as Dido was gearing up for the release of *No Angel*, 'Thank You' was heard by Mark 'The 45 King' James – one of the producers of Eminem's third album *The Marshall Mathers LP* (2000). He recorded a segment from his TV and sent it to the rapper, who was searching for samples to use on his astonishing metanarrative of murderous obsession, 'Stan'. In the interim, *No Angel* was given a US release where, thanks to 'Here With Me's prominence on one of the most watched series of the year, Dido was fast gaining nationwide recognition.

Mathers's decision to use a snippet of 'Thank You's first verse was one of many strokes of genius that studded his otherwise turbulent early career. It added a genuinely haunting extra-dimensional quality to 'Stan', a song that ranks among his greatest work. Even now my cerebral cortex, upon hearing those lines, serves up images from the video to 'Stan': rain lashing the windows; jagged pencil scrawls on cheap paper; dozens of torn Slim Shadies staring down from the wall.[23] 'Stan' was released in November 2000 and went to number one across the world, launching Dido from relative unknown to international superstar. Two million copies of *No Angel* were sold in America – and 300,000 in the UK – before she'd even released a single from it. It led Armstrong to wonder, in a January 2001 *Guardian* interview – which was undertaken before she'd played a single promotional show in the UK – what percentage of her enormous new fanbase was simply made up of 'Eminem fans looking a bit puzzled'.[24] While David Gray, Travis and Coldplay were all vying for everyman territory at this point, Dido was fast becoming the undisputed holder of the everywoman crown – 'or at least' as *The Telegraph* had it in 2004, 'every-suburban-twentysomething-English-girl-next-door'.

[22] As it happened, Arista ended up releasing the US edition of 'No Angel'.
[23] Dido also starred in the video to 'Stan', as the titular character's doomed girlfriend.
[24] This quote is typical of Dido who, across her career, unfailingly presents as self-effacing and funny.

'Here With Me', *No Angel*'s opening track and perhaps the album's best, is still effortlessly recognisable.[25] Armstrong's sweetly frivolous description of it as a 'post-shag song' does the song a slight disservice: it is also a stirring depiction of longing, swirled with the potency of new love. The opening lines of third single 'Hunter', backed only by acoustic guitar, provide a neat contrast to 'Here With Me's final throes, and the chorus, which speaks of moving forward in life, seeing the world 'alone again', are quietly and affectingly determined – much like Dido herself. The chorus of 'Don't Think of Me' boasts an angsty rush which pushes her closer to the territory staked out by Alanis Morissette, Natalie Imbruglia and Meredith Brooks in the late nineties – and while Dido didn't hit as hard musically as that trio, there is an envious bite to 'Don't Think of Me' that still leaves a mark today. 'Thank You's downbeat verses are given a redemptive, major-key escape that they never attain on 'Stan' – a source of disapproval to critics at the time, many of whom found the album's tasteful arrangements difficult to swallow. But *No Angel* is a well-constructed, eminently listenable and surprisingly varied record – some distance away from the winsome watercolours for which Dido is so often attributed. As Chris Martin was about to realise on Coldplay's *Parachutes*, Dido also identified that lyrical economy was key to creating songs that felt in some way 'universal'. But her frequent mentions of the domestic – cold cups of tea, unmade beds, missed buses – would prove divisive. To some, they lent her creations a comforting, relatable air, while others bemoaned her lack of risk-taking. Much like David Gray's best-loved album, we are now so used to hearing snippets of *No Angel* on adverts, in taxis, on supermarket radios as we do the big shop, that the larger work from which these fragments are drawn is almost completely obscured. In time, *No Angel* suffered a similar fate to *The Man Who* and *White Ladder*, eventually breeding mild contempt through overfamiliarity. Yet for a public frazzled by millennium-mania, Dido's work evidently felt like an anchor in a world morphing beyond recognition.

---

[25] The song's credits tantalisingly list one 'P. Gabriel' as a writer – the man in question is in fact Pascal Gabriel, producer and writer for S'Express and Bomb the Bass, who went on to hone the post-punk atmospheres of both Wire and Debbie Harry's later output.

No Angel was staggeringly successful – it remains one of the biggest selling debuts by a solo female artist of all time. It spent six weeks at number one upon its initial release, and has cumulatively spent almost three years in the Top 100. It has since reportedly sold over 15 million copies worldwide. She toured the States again in June 2001, playing far bigger arenas this time than on previous visits, and supported by some familiar faces: Travis. It was a pairing that suggested this 'polite rock' was more like a cohesive movement than any of the acts involved might have considered. Much like David Gray and Travis had done, Dido now found herself making music for which there was a huge and growing public appetite. She won two Brit Awards – Best Female Solo Artist and Best British Album – in February 2002.[26] Between albums, she again collaborated with Faithless to release the excellent 'One Step Too Far', a song which edged her sound towards the dancefloor once more. However, when it came to recording the following year's *Life For Rent*, the Armstrong duo wisely didn't mess with what was evidently a winning formula. Lead single 'White Flag', another intricately sketched micro-drama, and the title track, gleaned another two Top Ten hits.

Life For Rent repeated *No Angel*'s trick of initial chart success followed by serious staying power. It was number one for ten weeks, and then stayed in the Top 100 for over a year. Then, after the promotion and touring of the album began to wind down, Dido did something very interesting: she stopped. Post-*Life For Rent*, the effects of life on the road were clearly beginning to take their toll, and she was left heartbroken by the end of the 7-year relationship with her fiancé Bob Page in 2002, as well as the death of her father. The latter event informed her third album, *Safe Trip Home* (2008), and her difficulty in performing such personal material reportedly informed her choice not to tour with the collection. In an interview with *Stereogum* in 2019, she recalls the moment she came to her decision: 'It was like nine years straight [on tour]. I was like, "You know what? I probably need to stop." I think it came to a natural end, and then I had absolutely no desire to go back out for a while

[26] She would go on to win two more in 2004. Unbelievably, the Best British Album prize was presented by then-Arsenal defender Sol Campbell – which must have been quite the experience for lifelong Gunners fan Armstrong. The pair were even rumoured to have dated briefly in later years.

… I didn't for fifteen years.' By the late 2000s, Dido had all but disappeared from public life, but the measured manner of that retreat – through choice, and at a time which suited her – is to be applauded. For others in this book, the glare of the spotlight would prove more difficult to reckon with.

2. Manchester's Lost Souls
Doves, Elbow and Twisted Nerve Records

Doves – *Lost Souls*
Elbow – *Asleep in the Back*
Badly Drawn Boy – *The Hour of Bewilderbeast*
Alfie – *If You Happy With You Need Do Nothing*

By 1997, it was becoming clear that Oasis – previously Manchester's working-class band *du jour* – were losing sight of their roots. A year earlier, Noel Gallagher had proclaimed 'This is history!' as the band took to the stage for the first of their two enormous shows at Knebworth House. 'Right here, right now. This is history.' It wasn't an exaggeration: the appearances caught the band at the apex of their popularity, playing to 250,000 people over the weekend, one of the biggest single-act concerts ever staged in the UK. But Noel's proclamation also contained a telling slice of self-knowledge: this was as good as it was ever going to get. You sense the rest of the band knew it, too. As Paul Arthurs, a.k.a. 'Bonehead' said in 2009, 'I always thought we should have bowed out after the second night at Knebworth.' The pressure to recreate the inspiration found on *Definitely Maybe* (1994) and *(What's the Story) Morning Glory?* (1995) was proving unbearable, and that apex became a tipping point. Suddenly, Oasis had become the over-evolved sauropods of British music: enormous, lumbering and likely to cause damage if you left them in a small room together. The sinking of an engine-less Silver Shadow Rolls-Royce into a swimming pool for the cover artwork of the band's third studio album *Be Here Now* (1997) encapsulated this decadence perfectly; in Daniel Rachel's *Don't Look Back in Anger*, Noel acknowledges the band were forgetting their common touch. 'I couldn't write for the man in the street, because I wasn't the man in the street.'

The breathlessly anticipated release of *Be Here Now* was a lead story on the BBC's six o'clock news, complete with footage of punters queuing outside a megastore at opening time,[27] hoping to secure their purchase of what would surely be a masterpiece from 'the greatest band in the world... since The Beatles.' Yet the reality of the album was very different. At a bloated 71 minutes long, and

[27] One of whom was a young Peter Doherty – more of him later.

51

with an eight-minute lead single in the shape of 'D'You Know What I Mean?', it neatly encapsulated what Britpop had become by this point: overinflated, self-satisfied, and no longer very much fun at all. Although *Be Here Now* was another commercial success, a fractious Radio 1 interview with Steve Lamacq was just one of many indications that the band, and by extension, Britpop, was beginning to implode before our eyes. While the Gallaghers set off on their sprawling world tour to promote the album (with Travis in tow), the way was becoming clear for the next Great Manchester Band.

While the wider world seemed knotty and in flux, the late nineties saw the fortuitous intertwining of a loose collective of creators based in and around Manchester, many of whom played a part in each other's musical stories. Doves, Elbow, Andy Votel, Damon Gough, Alfie, I Am Kloot, Jane Weaver and dozens of other visual artists, DJs and promoters provided the impetus for a huge shift in the city's musical atmosphere. An early Andy Votel 7" release, featuring both Jane Weaver and Doves, wittily owns this interconnectedness with its title: 'Everyone Knows Everyone Else'. Yet two groups were destined to pull away from the rest. Doves and Elbow had already been honing their respective crafts for most of the nineties, and with *Lost Souls* and *Asleep in the Back* they crafted twin debut masterpieces that defined the feel of the era, moving the city's musical narrative forward once again. They had bold visions of a very different Manchester as it emerged from the pile-up of baggy and Britpop: their music wove beautiful poetry from the everyday, but it was also mournful, damaged and weird. Arriving in the early noughties, it felt strikingly relevant to a generation struggling to define themselves in both the din of the millennium celebrations, and the enormous musical shadows left by the recent past.

★★★

'We were all at school together, in various rock bands, with The Smiths and New Order always looming large … just messing around, really,' says Doves drummer and vocalist Andy Williams.[28] Little did he know then that, alongside twin brother Jez and their classmate, Jimi Goodwin, the trio were starting down a path, begun in the mid-eighties, that would see them make music together for nearly three decades. The trio split after school, and briefly went their separate ways, but they were brought back together by rave. 'We'd actually lost touch with Jimi after school – and then we bumped into each other again at The Haçienda. Dance culture came along at just the right time for all of us.' After school, the boys had 'tried all the retail and dead-end jobs … we were basically unemployable'. So they did what any self-respecting clubbers did at the time: they made a record. It was to be the beginning of a remarkable journey.

[28] Author interview with Andy Williams, September 2019. All subsequent quotes from this interview unless otherwise stated.

Christening themselves Sub Sub, the trio produced the single 'Space Face', a bracing techno workout, in the brothers' bedroom, releasing it as a white label in 1991. Williams compares the process, rightly, to the early years of punk: 'We basically put £200 each in and sold it out of the back of a car, driving to record stores, shifting a few copies and trying to play at clubs or raves wherever we ended up.' Sub Sub's advertising was equally rudimentary: 'We just put our phone number on the sleeve so shops could call us up.' 'Space Face' was an underground hit, and saw them picked up by Ten Records, a Virgin imprint. Ten put out an official 12" of 'Space Face', but Sub Sub were dropped shortly afterwards – casualties of the transitory, singles-based nature of dance culture at the time. 'We kind of thought it was all over at that point … that's when [former Joy Division/New Order manager] Rob Gretton picked us up,' says Williams – the first of several redemptive episodes in the band's twisty story. Dave Rofe – Doves' manager, who has worked with the band since the Sub Sub days – was beginning his career and met Jimi through a friend. He was working in Gretton's office at the time, 'answering the phone if needed, but working on bits and pieces of my own as a fledgling manager'. Rofe introduced Sub Sub to Gretton at Dry, the bar owned by Factory Records. Liking what he saw and heard of them, Gretton offered the band a 50/50, 'Factory-style' deal on his new label, Rob's Records. The first release on the imprint was the *Coast EP*, offered originally to Virgin, but which they had declined to release. *Coast* performed 'modestly', according to Rofe, but then came a moment of inspiration: using a sample from an old disco record that Andy had won at a fairground, the band began working on a new track that needed a big, powerful soul vocal. They played the track to Temper Temper's Melanie Williams, a friend of Goodwin's, who duly obliged; the result was the euphoric 'Ain't No Love (Ain't No Use)'. The song was unexpectedly and emphatically successful – a true crossover hit that reached number three in the charts in April 1993, as well as earning heavy rotation on the club circuit. 'We're forever grateful to that song because it meant we didn't have to get proper jobs,' says Williams, the hint of a smile in his voice. Yet there was always more to Sub Sub than their infectious singles. Even before the formation of Doves, Goodwin and the Williams brothers were evolving their sound far beyond the beat-driven efforts of their early days. A cursory listen to Sub Sub's only official UK album *Full Fathom Five* (1994)[29] reveals a sonic palette far more nuanced than the average dance outfit – and let's not forget, there were *a lot* of average dance acts around at the time. It is a patchy listen today, but contains recognisable elements of trip-hop, jazz and ambient, already suggesting ambition far beyond the dancefloor. And though Williams confesses to dissatisfaction with both Sub Sub records, the sense of a band working away on their own terms is still palpable.

Then, famously, disaster struck: in February 1996, on the Williams' birthday, Sub Sub's studio in Ancoats was all but destroyed in a ruinous fire, along with virtually everything the band had been working on. It was an event that Andy describes as 'Ground Zero' for the band, leaving them with a stark choice: give up entirely, or start again from scratch. Choosing to view the incident as a clean break rather than a full stop, they regrouped, although they wouldn't rename themselves until a little later. Settling on the more song-oriented sound hinted at on some of the later Sub Sub material, and using remnants of surviving songs, the band began work again. As Jez would tellingly write on Twitter some twenty years later: 'This was a calling to do something that was ANTI-BRITPOP.' In another development that retrospectively looks like a baton being passed, Gretton suggested they use the studio then owned by New Order, VIBE, in Cheetham Hill. It's no exaggeration to say that Doves were literally playing amongst the ruins of an earlier Manchester. Andy recalled the setup for Q in 2009:

> It was a pretty oppressive place with no windows and thieves trying to break in! But it was also an inspiring place to be as it belonged to New Order and we were fans … The garage there was full of their old gear; it was full of vintage keyboards, sequencers, drum machines and was like some weird techno graveyard in there. I also remember finding Stephen Morris's Rogers drum kit that he used in Joy Division stuffed behind some knackered flight case.

[29] A second album, 1998's *Delta Tapes,* was mystifyingly only released in Portugal and Australia.

Fittingly for a band attempting resurrection, one of the songs on their debut release as a new outfit was called 'Rise'. With Gretton's help, Doves, as they were now named, released the *Cedar EP* in December 1998 on their own label, Casino Records; it was named *NME*'s single of the week. Things appeared to be moving once more for the band, but then, tragedy struck again: just a week before the release of their next effort, the *Sea EP* in May 1999, Gretton suffered a fatal heart attack at the age of just 46. He was a titan of Manchester music, whose passing felt like another door closing on history. The release went ahead, with grief and uncertainty overshadowing another round of positive reviews. Bigger record companies now began to circle the band – but with Gretton's death still fresh in everyone's minds, a measure of sensitivity was required in any talks. Jeff Barrett, co-founder of Heavenly Recordings (newly an imprint of EMI at the time), remembers the caution with which they made their initial approach:

> Rob incredibly sadly and prematurely passed away just as Doves had finished their debut album. We waited for an appropriate period of mourning, then approached Rob's widow, Lesley, and asked if we could talk to the group. There'd been other interest in the group – some others didn't show quite the decorum we did [after Rob's death] – but when we want something we don't mess around or let anyone else get a look in, really … We'd just done our deal with EMI and they were the first thing we'd brought in … Suddenly I had the attention of everyone in that building who didn't get much of a thrill from working with Robbie Williams or Geri Halliwell.

Doves' debut album, which Barrett describes as 'a masterpiece', finally arrived in April 2000. It was worth the wait.

Lost Souls is a record of striking and relentless density, its claustrophobic atmosphere and long run-time obviously the product of artists working in prolonged containment. Keyboardist and sound manipulator Martin Rebelski – who also joined Doves on tour, and was to all intents and purposes the fourth member of the band – provided the oppressive atmospherics that drive many of the album's key moments. Brooding opener 'Firesuite' is a fine example of this: as one of the only surviving tracks from the Sub Sub days, it neatly bridges the gap between the two eras. The song's unnerving samples include a girl intoning 'hello…?' The first 'lost soul' of the album, perhaps. Heavily treated vocals and stuttering guitars give the effect of musicians stirring from dormancy, uncurling their limbs and testing for range.

'Firesuite' boasts an unhurried menace that stalks much of the opening half of the album. On 'Break Me Gently', Williams gives way to Jimi Goodwin on vocals – it was in fact Jimi's first ever attempt at a lead vocal. Again, the song is built around a sighing vocal loop and Rebelski's textures, closing out with a sampled answer-machine message from someone who is, to put it mildly, not too pleased by the caller's absence. Another lost soul flickering through. And still they come, whispering over 'Sea Song' – the first track on *Lost Souls* where Goodwin's vocals are presented largely without treatment, though they are fed through a Hammond organ speaker here. Even twenty years after first hearing them, they remain spine-tingling. There's something in those scuffed, bristling 's's and elongated flourishes that uniquely decorate the end of his lines, as if the words are too big for his throat, anxious to be released. They are on full show throughout the central trio of songs on *Lost Souls*, comprising 'Sea Song', 'Rise' and the title track: deliciously drawn-out jams, crucial to establishing the tone of the record, and long enough that you too begin to feel disorientated.

'Melody Calls' ushers in the more anthemic second side of *Lost Souls*, consolidated by the single 'Catch the Sun', whose urgency and accessibility stands in contrast to what has gone before. Its straightforwardness is deceptive, however: 'Catch the Sun' nearly didn't make the album at all, as the band struggled to find the right method of recording it (five distinct versions are available online). 'The Man Who Told Everything', which became a Top 40 single the following October, is the least complicated 'verse-chorus' song on the album, telling the story of a whistleblower preparing his escape after selling a story to the press. It encapsulates the mood of *Lost Souls*: euphoria tempered by needling, caustic anxiety. Perhaps this was how Manchester felt at the time – crowded with the casualties of hedonism, fading fast, hounded by a chorus of regrets.

> I had a book of short ghost stories as a kid and there was one chapter called 'The White Lady' about an old inn where the ghost would come to visit guests in the dead of night. The story really spooked me as a kid and I always remember the room where the haunting took place: the cedar room.

'The Cedar Room' sits near the end of this collection not as an afterthought, but as a revelation. *Lost Souls* is a haunting, and Andy Williams's childhood nightmare, the Cedar Room, its epicentre – a place where this gathering of phantoms can find fleeting release from the earth that binds them. With its colossal drumbeat and ecstatic chorus, 'The Cedar Room' is also the closest Doves come to the scale and intentions of their Britpop forbears. There's a lovely section after the final chorus where the band simply *plays*, revelling in what they've created. Goodwin croons the song home, and Doves ascent is complete. But there is more, and it feels fitting that the final sounds we hear on *Lost Souls* are those of crackling embers, at the end of 'A House'. Goodwin's vocals were recorded on a dictaphone, and it feels like a message to the past: a fleeting, elegiac nod to their former selves. The whole album also acted as a memorial of sorts to Gretton – lost before he got a chance to see the band rise again.

Lost Souls was a critical hit, with future Q editor Ted Kessler's 9/10 review in *NME* perhaps paying the ultimate compliment: 'Doves may not have any of the attitude, youth or sartorial influence of their forebears but, by God, they make being sad after drugs sound great.'[30] Within that quote is another interesting nod to those Manchester giants that still 'loomed large'. By this stage, says Williams, the club scene in particular 'had gone really sour … there was a lot of violence around'. Where Sub Sub had provided the soundtrack to going out, *Lost Souls,* despite its occasional moments of transcendence, was music for comedown and retreat.

Doves toured throughout 2000 and 2001, and sales built nicely, far surpassing the band's expectations: 'We thought it would sell 10,000 copies or something,' Jez Williams told Alex Petridis in a *Guardian* interview in 2002. At the time of that article's writing, it had sold

---

[30] An *NME* cover appearance for the band that year, photographed holding their avian namesakes, hailed 'The Birth of The Coo'.

160,000. Further evidence of the band's critical standing arrived in the shape of a Mercury Prize nomination. In an odd turn of events, they were effectively nominated twice: Doves were close friends of Damon Gough, a.k.a. Badly Drawn Boy, and the band had served as a backing on some of his early singles. They also played on elements of Gough's debut album *The Hour of Bewilderbeast*, which ended up beating *Lost Souls* to that year's prize. Williams recalls 'we never expected to win, so Damon winning was a victory for us too in a way … [*Bewilderbeast*] came as a surprise to everyone.'

The critical adoration, as well as the Mercury nod for *Lost Souls*, had 'put the wind in our sails', and by 2002 there was palpable anticipation for new Doves material. What they did next was slightly unexpected: after heavily trailing their new single 'There Goes the Fear', Heavenly then announced that it would be released and deleted on the same day, 15th April 2002. It was the ultimate limited edition – a one-day only offer that would be completely unattemptable in today's digital environment. It proved an effective stunt, supplying Doves with their second number three single, ten years after 'Ain't No Love…' reached the same position. 'There Goes the Fear' was an instant classic, condensing everything the band had been working towards since the Sub Sub days: a propulsive beat, a memorable chorus and a vivid, frequently unexpected instrumental palette. The album version even features that least indie of instruments, the Brazilian *cuíca*, or 'laughing gourd', in an extended percussive coda. It suggested musicians riding high on confidence – a feeling only reinforced when their second album, *The Last Broadcast*, arrived.

Where *Lost Souls* had carefully built to an exhilarating conclusion, *The Last Broadcast* began near the top, and kept pushing. The vertiginous riff of 'Words' felt like a logical progression from 'The Cedar Room's bombast. The introduction of a gospel choir on 'Satellites' was as natural as recording parts of 'M62 Song' underneath a motorway bridge. And the oversaturated melancholy of tracks like 'Where We're Calling From' and 'Friday's Dust' was ritually blasted away by the muscle of 'N.Y.' and 'Pounding'. Here, finally, was a band comfortable and confident enough to reveal every side of themselves at once. Again, they saved the album's finest song until the end: 'Caught by the River' was an anthemic call to life, aimed at someone intent on leaving it. Yet it also feels gloriously and personally redemptive. If 'A House' was a humble act of mourning, was 'Caught by the River' Doves thanking the gods for their second chance?

Whatever their intentions, *The Last Broadcast* brought the acclaim that its immediacy demanded, and it duly reached number one in the album charts.[31] 'Pounding' and 'Caught by the River', both post-album releases, continued what was to become an unbroken five-year run of Top 40 singles. In their 8.0 review, *Pitchfork* praised the album's detail, calling it 'an easy record to come back to – chances are you missed an awful lot the first few times you listened'. High praise, and also a strong sign that ears were also being turned on the other side of the Atlantic. After two decades of Northern turbulence, Doves finally seemed set fair. They have always boasted a uniquely beguiling vocabulary; with *Lost Souls* and *The Last Broadcast*, they found its richest and clearest expression.

★★★

---

[31] It was to be the first of two successive number ones: their third, *Some Cities*, also hit the top spot in February 2005.

I met Guy Garvey once. I was on holiday in 2002 in Cornwall with my family, at the age when I was still buying handfuls of CD singles every Monday. That week, while the rest of my family picked their way along Truro's main shopping street, I shuffled off to HMV to buy my own sonic groceries – including Elbow's new single, 'Fallen Angel'. I saw an interesting poster in there, too, which got me thinking. On my way back to meet up with the rest of the Clayton cohort, I ducked into a stationers' shop and bought a permanent marker.

Later that week, we visited The Eden Project, where I'd spotted that Elbow were due to play that evening, supporting PJ Harvey. I stuffed my new single and marker into my satchel, along with some formless hope of running into a member of the band so they could inscribe my wares. The day itself could hardly be called fruitless – I did, after all, see a lot of exotic produce. But by the time I'd pondered over buying a pen made from recycled plastic in the gift shop,[32] all I could boast from the day was a brief glance of Polly Jean as she dashed from one biome to another. My parents signalled they were heading back to the car park while I, ever the optimist, said I would hang around for another five minutes before joining them up there. Further mooching ensued, and eventually I gave up. Trudging back up the gravel path, past the specially-constructed stage, I brushed past a tall bloke and continued on my way. Then a hundred yards later, my brain caught up with my legs, I performed a swift about-turn and shouted 'Guy!' in my half-broken squeaky-teen voice. I can only imagine what Garvey must have thought as a breathless, gawky stripling caught him up, started rummaging around in his satchel, produced a CD single and a permanent marker, and shyly asked if 'you could possibly sign this Guy please, I'd be really grateful'. He was, of course, charming. A bit bemused – remember, this was pre-Mercury Prize, pre-national treasure-era Elbow – but all too happy to oblige me. Since then, I've bought rarer music and collected more obscure signatures, but that single remains a modest treasure of which I'm very proud. Little did I or the band know that, by then, they were standing on the precipice of greatness.

Earlier that year, Elbow had played *Top of the Pops* for the first time, on an episode that aired the day after Valentine's Day (and was therefore filmed on the day itself). They performed 'Asleep in the Back' – a song initially omitted from their debut album of the same name, and now included as part of the tracklist in a newly updated edition. 'It's a waltz … partner up,' says Garvey with a sly smile. Later in the song, Garvey breaks away from his mic stand to 'conduct' the brass section at the back (a gaggle reportedly made up of invited friends of the band). As the song sways to a close, the *TOTP* graphic flashes up with the number 19. It was the first time Elbow had cracked not only the Top 40, but the Top *Twenty*. It felt like vindication for a band that truly deserved it.

Even if the story had ended there, with Elbow goofing around on the nation's premier pop music show, and a blossoming reputation as purveyors of fine love songs, it might have been enough. Yet

[32] Any eco-friendliness this trip might have instilled in me unfortunately did not prevent the purchase of many thousands more jewel-case CDs.

the band now find themselves in a rare position: respected, even adored by both indie fans and the wider listening public, they also command serious critical attention – and boast, in Garvey, a genuine star. Of their contemporaries, only Coldplay have outdone Elbow's reputational and commercial success. Yet while Chris Martin and co. consistently stretch the scope of their lyrics, arrangements and resultant audience further outwards with each new release, Elbow's has been a pattern of repeated homecomings. No matter how big their profile has become, they have built their world on the solid foundations of the everyday, drawing from the same well of experience that they have since the beginning. And that beginning is longer ago than you might expect.

Elbow famously took ten years to make their debut album, *Asleep in the Back*. But that's because they weren't really Elbow at all. Meeting at Bury College in the late eighties, the members that would go on to form the band originally started in two: RPM, which contained Mark Potter, Pete Turner and Richard Jupp; and Synoptic Reverb, featuring Guy Garvey and Craig Potter.[33] The two bands merged and changed their name to Mr Soft, zeroing in on a totally un-Elbow-like sound: funk. Influenced by Sly and the Family Stone and Parliament, they played gigs in Bury without making any serious inroads. Even a name change, to the no-less-terrible 'Soft', didn't result in an upturn in fortunes. Despite their minimal impact on Bury's music scene, Soft continued to hone their craft, and their disciplined attitude to rehearsal resulted in a collection of songs that would eventually coalesce into the Elbow sound. Guy Garvey's love of both complex prog rock and sophisticated pop, thrust upon him at home via the tastes of his five older sisters, was beginning to come to the fore. The band built up a reputation at venues like the Night & Day Café on Oldham Street, and the Roadhouse on Newton Street (where some of the band were also employed), both stalwart venues of Manchester's Northern Quarter. They ditched Soft for good in 1997, in favour of Elbow. The name comes from a scene in Dennis Potter's 1986 BBC series *The Singing Detective*, in which a character describes 'elbow' as 'the most sensual word in the English language'.

[33] Allow me to direct you at this point to Mick Middles's excellent history of the band, *Reluctant Heroes: The Story of Elbow* (Omnibus, 2009).

From this point, things began to ramp up: they played 1998's In The City convention,[34] catching the eye of Island Records. In what must have been a surreal few months after years of slog, Island bankrolled the sessions for Elbow's first album, ploughing £250,000 into the band's development. Yet almost immediately there was another setback to endure. Just as the band had completed their studio time, Island were bought out by Universal – and in the resultant upheaval, Elbow cruelly fell between the cracks. They were dropped, left sitting on an album's worth of unreleasable material and probably wondering what the hell had just happened. Undeterred, they released two EPs on the independent label Ugly Man, slowly building the buzz again. The Ugly Man releases caught the ear of John Peel, and the resulting exposure helped them sign up to V2 (ironically also part of the Universal group), in 2001. They re-recorded their debut with Ben Hillier, reportedly feeling freer and more relaxed. Not many bands get the opportunity for a do-over, after all – and Elbow were thankful for their second chance. Recalling the sessions for *Uncut* in 2014, Garvey says 'It was a case of, "Fuck it, we can do what we want", whereas the first time it was a case of, "This has got to be perfect". Lots of fun and experimentation.' The result was a languid, coiled confidence that permeates every note of *Asleep in the Back.*

For Elbow fans drawn to their anthemic, post-*Seldom Seen Kid* output, a song like 'Any Day Now' would probably come as a surprise. It practically sleepwalks out of the speakers, with Pete Turner's dub-inflected bass dominating the mix. Guy Garvey's vocal is buried under huge drifts of keyboard and organ, then joined in the chorus by an unnerving glassy-eyed chant. Immediately, the listener understands this is a band unafraid to wait – they'd already been doing so for a decade, after all. 'Any Day Now' also begins to establish some of *Asleep in the Back*'s themes. Thwarted attempts at escape; the claustrophobia of loneliness; the myopia of addiction… it's a world away from 'One Day Like This'. The early single, 'Red', is a warning song – the story of a friend or lover told from the perspective of a concerned onlooker whose helplessness is reflected in the sighing strings that drape the song's chorus ('you're a tragedy starting to happen'). 'Red' is also the first track on which we get a true idea of Garvey's vocal power – an

[34] More of which later.

asset that Elbow would fully utilise in their later work. And if 'Red' is the perfect vocal showcase, 'Little Beast' demonstrates Garvey's considerable lyrical prowess – a fragment like 'slide in shadow cobble-creep' hardly typical of your average indie tearaways. He reflected on the song for *Drowned in Sound* in 2009:

> When there's nothing to do in a small town apart from what's expected of you, you can get caught up in it all. My favourite lyric is 'the whole town's dripping down a hill like the spine of something dead'. There's actually a mill town north of Bury where the street layout looks like the spine of a dinosaur coming over the hill.

There's a surreal bent to much of Garvey's early writing, which prompted comparisons with another great northern outsider: Mark E. Smith. But where The Fall's cryptic transmissions were nearly always delivered via stark and skeletal music, it takes some digging through the dense strata of *Asleep in the Back* to reveal Elbow's oddness. 'Powder Blue' is a depiction of nightmarish co-dependency, with a lover, or a drug, or a city. (Elbow skilfully remind us that the three are not so different.) 'Bitten by the Tailfly' is another northern night-portrait, this time narrated by a lothario on the pull. The title track arrives next, its sparkling waltz-time arrangement revealing the tender side of Elbow: generous, apologetic, rueful.[35] But 'Newborn', the most prog-influenced song on the album, is a different prospect altogether. Initially a delicate conversation between Garvey and the rest of his band, the first three minutes of the song unfold with a grace that earlier efforts had only hinted at. It's a quality that Garvey attributes to an unlikely source – Phil Collins-era Genesis:

> I read somewhere about a guy who called himself a music psychologist. He reckoned that the stuff that you listen to between the ages eight and eleven has the most influence on you. In my case it's true. I used to sing along to Peter Gabriel's solo records during that time. I thought that he was amazing. The first Phil Collins album has a song that is the musical blueprint for 'Newborn'. It's a song called 'Entangled'.

[35] After being omitted from the original pressing, 'Asleep in the Back' was added to a reissued version in February 2002.

One listen to 'Entangled', from Genesis' first post-Peter Gabriel album *A Trick of the Tail* (1976), confirms the songs are musical relatives.[36] Sung by Collins, but written by Steve Hackett and Tony Banks, its guitars share the same lulling, careful mood as the first half of 'Newborn'. But where 'Entangled' entrances, 'Newborn' explodes: the monumental organ line which connects the two sections is suddenly and brutally replaced with a hurricane of guitars, as Garvey howls his band off a cliff. What still thrills about 'Newborn' is how *heavy* it is, closer to metal than anything else. The words double their pace too, pouring out like rainwater from a burst dam. Then, just as fiercely as it rages, it screeches to a halt with a sharp industrial crunch. The levity of 'Don't Mix Your Drinks' feels necessary at this point, its voice seeming to come from an older and wiser place, its guitars like rain ghosting at pub windows. 'Coming Second' then delivers another shock with a shuddering, bitter groove – closer to the gloomy shadows of *Mezzanine* or *Leftism* than any of Elbow's guitar-wielding peers. 'Scattered Black and Whites' closes the album sweetly: dappled drums, a fragile cascade of guitar, interlaced with lyrics that speak of finding shelter, if only in memories. There are troubled voices everywhere on *Asleep in the Back* – much like the ghostly cast of *Lost Souls* – and it seems right that some of them should experience peace at last.

Elbow's dense atmospherics and penchant for an outsider perspective led to inevitable comparisons with Doves,[37] but in truth they were the only two bands at the time making music like each other – a kind of dual anomaly. Speaking with *Nothing but Hope and Passion* in 2016, Garvey compared the two sounds:

> Just like Doves we came from a sample culture. They were big with those whole dance / Haçienda scenes while we preferred the Bristol-sound of trip-hop bands like Massive Attack and Tricky; the stuff that came out of the back of acid jazz. Those clear and partly stoned grooves inspired songs like 'Any Day Now' on the LP. DJ Shadow's early stuff was also very inspirational for us.

---

[36] Garvey would later meet Gabriel for the first time while Elbow recorded at his Real World studio in Box, Wiltshire. Cringing in a 2005 interview for *Magnet*, he recalls having a spoon balanced on his nose just as his hero walked in to greet the band at dinner.

[37] In a 2020 interview with Jools Holland, Garvey describes Doves as being 'the year above us' in terms of life experience. The slight age gap is telling, and meant the two bands ended up with very different 'lifestyle choices': Doves the club veterans, Elbow the wizened barflies.

Elbow drew from trip-hop, but also from a palette of sounds not really heard since Talk Talk's *Spirit of Eden* era or Bark Psychosis' 1994 post-rock masterpiece *Hex*. Garvey's vocals have always drawn comparison with Peter Gabriel's, and they are certainly similar. But where Gabriel's voice soars effortlessly over the top of his arrangements, Garvey's seem to be mined from a deep and troubled place, especially on *Asleep in the Back*. That's not to suggest they are overwrought: he simply wears his lyrics with pride, like a boxer's belt after a tough fight.

With their debut collection, Elbow had found a way to evoke the best and worst of human life in a way that felt organic and unpretentious, while attempting textures and atmospherics several levels above their contemporaries. It drew admiring looks from critics, but the lack of a big single meant that, for now, Elbow were only able to reach the level of indie darlings. *The Guardian* praised Garvey's 'fertile mind' in a four-star review, and *Pitchfork* described 'a skilled and laudable debut. *Asleep in the Back* finds them starting their recording career … at a level a lot of bands don't even reach on their third or fourth albums.' Despite their early stumble, Elbow were now beginning to reap the kind of rewards Garvey must have envisioned as he slogged around Bury with Mr Soft.

The adage that you have ten years to write your first album, and six months to write your second, held more than true for Elbow. Yet when the time came, they seemed to relish the challenge. The follow-up to *Asleep in the Back*, 2003's *Cast of Thousands* (so called because their Glastonbury 2002 crowd sings 'we still believe in love, so fuck you' on 'Grace Under Pressure') began to see them open out in every direction. The most immediate difference is in the production: a patina of sonic gloom is lifted away, and the effect is like the restoration of an old building. Nakedly emotional songs like 'Switching Off' and 'Fugitive Motel' are given space to breathe, and are all the more astonishing for it. *Cast of Thousands* also marks the point at which Elbow began to reach more consciously for the epic, shedding much of their tendency towards knotty prog rock. 'Grace Under Pressure' is the best example, but opener 'Ribcage', with its gospel choir and dramatic dynamics, also suggested a band with newly sustained control of their artistic voice.

Elbow's growing reputation meant increased time on the road, presenting Guy Garvey with a fresh well of feeling to draw from. Where *Asleep in the Back* had been preoccupied with the claustrophobic effects of small-town life, a significant portion of *Cast of Thousands* dealt with the opposite: homesickness, longing for the comfort of community. 'I blow you a kiss / it should reach you tomorrow', from 'Fugitive Motel', surely one of the most succinct and affecting depictions of touring hardship yet penned. For all its grand ambition, however, *Cast of Thousands* still boasts moments of almost unbearable intimacy. 'Switching Off' is agonisingly precise in its description of a life drawing to a close; 'Buttons and Zips', portrays fumbled love in a 'blossom shed' which, coupled with a close-recorded vocal from Garvey, is almost blush-worthy. Again, the press found warm words for the album, amid the inevitable comparisons to Coldplay and Radiohead. Yet there was also a sense that Elbow were carving a singular path for themselves, in what was by now a crowded market: *Uncut*'s review called them 'human where Radiohead are impenetrable, but complex where Coldplay are banal … unquantifiably great'.

Cast of Thousands would have represented a career peak for many lesser bands. Yet for Elbow it was simply the next in a remarkable run of records, serving to steadily build their reputation even before *The Seldom Seen Kid* put them over the top. The title of their third album, *Leaders of the Free World* (2005), might have suggested a heavy-handed political effort, and while that was true of the title track, it also contained some of their loveliest and most disarming portraits yet. 'Mexican Standoff' is particularly interesting, a keyed-up fight song that continues the band's ability to break up passages of pleasantness with something more toothsome. 'Forget Myself', perhaps their most conventional single to date, still managed to kick harder than anything they'd done before. *Leaders of the Free World* also contained one indisputable masterpiece. Tucked away at the back of the album is 'Great Expectations', a gentle waltz which deftly reframes and subverts the image of a white wedding, moving it to a northern night bus. A grizzled drunk is the witnessing priest; the aisle is thronged with 'Stockport supporter's club', who 'kindly supplied us a choir'. It is Garvey at his best; writing that feels like sorcery.

Elbow's is a vision that, no matter how epic the framing, is always anchored by real life. They don't often indulge in the cosmic, because Garvey is a portrait artist at heart; a trait that harks back to his days of sketching and note-taking in Bury market as a teenager. Would the young Guy ever believe his voice would one day be used on the city's tram announcement system, as it was in September 2019, for the BBC's Music Day? Or that the bells of the town hall would ever chime to the tune of 'One Day Like This'? Let's be thankful he had the courage to throw those curtains wider, embracing the world, while hugging those closest to him even tighter. We are lucky to have him.

★★★

The year 2000, as well as signalling the dawn of a new millennium, also heralded two daunting personal shifts. The first was universal: that autumn I started at 'big school' and, as it does for so many kids, my life changed irreversibly. Having been a relatively big fish in primary school, almost immediately I was relegated to minnow status: split up from my old friends, navigating a school the size of a small town, all the while figuring out what the hell a protractor was, and why I needed one. What's more, the pursuit I'd found I excelled in (drama) was viewed as desperately uncool by my new peers, many of whom seemed to actively *enjoy* rugby union. I was beginning to realise the same thing every early teen does, after moving from a school of a couple of hundred to well over a thousand: that my little corner of the world was crushingly insignificant. Those humdrum adolescent worries played out alongside a more painful change, too: my father, who has suffered from severe MS for most of his adult life, took a sharp downward turn during this period – his mobility decreasing from walking stick to wheelchair in a frighteningly short space of time. My younger sister and I watched on helplessly as my parents scrambled to adjust to his rapidly worsening symptoms. He spent extended periods in hospital. As a result, we spent a lot of time in the car after school; or in waiting rooms, snacking from vending machines; or at his bedside. Perhaps, as the first Christmas of the new millennium approached, it was no wonder I began to look inwards.

It was around this time I bought an album called *The Hour of Bewilderbeast*.[38] I knew it had just won some prize or other. And I also knew it was written and played by a bloke called Damon who wore a tea-cosy on his head. I did not – could not – know the well of solace that awaited within.

If David Gray was an improbable chart-topper, Damon Michael Gough was an even less likely critical darling, and his career as Badly Drawn Boy remains one of British music's most enigmatic stories. It's a tale wrapped up inextricably with that of the label he co-owned with Andy Votel, Twisted Nerve Records, who flourished as one of the most respected indies of the period. Votel, whose real name is Andrew Shallcross, was already an established artist and DJ by the time the millennium approached – his pseudonym is a reference to Violators of the English Language, a hip-hop collective he was a member of in the late eighties. He then spent the nineties both making and collecting music of all kinds, spinning an enviable smorgasbord of jazz, psych, krautrock and everything else in between, at The Haçienda and myriad other clubs and bars across Manchester. By the end of the decade, he was a regular DJ at the Night & Day Café, where he would present 'monthly Morricone themed nights and Krautrock sessions'.[39]

Votel met Damon Gough by chance, and in unlikely circumstances: 'He introduced himself while hearing me DJ in a bar, and asked me if I wanted some stickers printing at his dad's factory!' It was the start of a friendship that would bear fruit for many years. Votel also remembers the northern malaise that characterised the immediate

---

[38] On CD this time, from MVC (RIP).
[39] Author interview with Andy Votel, February 2020. All subsequent quotes from this interview unless otherwise stated.

years after Britpop: 'We arrived during a miserable pop-cultural void in Manchester, and we were thrown together like a reality TV gameshow.' He envisioned Twisted Nerve as an 'imaginary label', existing in parallel to, yet utterly distinct from, the city's dominant cultures. 'There was a definite yearning to denounce any current trends such as dance music or indie, mainly because those scenes were so prevalent in Manchester. In hindsight, I guess there was something of a throwback aesthetic to the initial roster, but only because we were in total denial of current trends, and we were using cheap equipment and making vinyl records and cassettes instead of CDs.' Such was the CD format's ubiquity at the time that 'Piccadilly had literally thrown out their 7" vinyl racking the week before the first [Twisted Nerve] record came out.'[40]

The label was a truly independent labour of love, with Votel also using his design skills to create and produce sleeves for his artists. The initial Twisted Nerve stable now had Gough at its core – although at this point there were few signs of the commercial riches that awaited:

> I genuinely had no expectations of his musical accessibility, all I knew or cared about was that it was like nothing else I'd heard, and I also knew that he was open minded and versatile within his minimal means … To be honest, if there had been any glaring indications of what people later considered as greatness then I probably would have stepped in the opposite direction, Manchester was very ego-driven at that point, the last thing we needed was more greatness!

Those minimal means spawned a cluster of intermittently superb EPs – simply numbered 1, 2 and 3, then followed by 1999's *It Came from the Ground* – the first of which is now vanishingly rare. These mumbled mini-collections served to introduce the world to perhaps the ultimate anti-Britpop artist. Yet in spite of the whimsical name, yards of corduroy and permanent beanie hat, Badly Drawn Boy was far from a novelty folk act: Gough, like previous lo-fi dabblers Robert Pollard and R. Stevie Moore, was a bona fide rock star simply using whatever equipment was available to him. His attitude to song structure – and

---

[40] The legendary Piccadilly Records, also on Oldham Street. I speak from personal experience when I assure you they have since reinstated their vinyl display units.

indeed, to the number of versions a song might reasonably have – was certainly offhand, but it was never slapdash; there is real art behind the apparent sketches of his early work. It's especially instructive to listen to both versions of 'Outside is a Light' from *It Came from the Ground*. The two iterations – one more polished, and one that sounds like it was recorded a thousand feet underwater – both feel necessary. Gough was making full use of the EP format as a proving ground for his own sounds and ideas, and his live appearances further fed into the murky mystique conjured by the recorded output.

Badly Drawn Boy shows were a world away from the polished swagger of his Britpop predecessors. Depending on your point of view, they were either endearingly or annoyingly erratic: he would amble through songs, often stopping halfway through, forgetting whole sections, or simply become bored and move on. *NME* described his performance at the Channel 4 *Barfly Sessions* as 'shambolic', and they weren't the only ones. In an interview with *UK Music Reviews* in 2010, Gough remembers the impact of his early stage presence:

> Back in the mid-nineties, if we are talking about Manchester, Oasis were the band, and at that time everybody in Manchester was trying to be the next Oasis. So when I sprang onto the scene as a guy with a guitar and a drum machine together with a Casio keyboard, handing out flowers, I rapidly earned the reputation as being shambolic … rightly so in a lot of cases, but I was also doing something a bit different and it got me noticed.

While clearly excited by Gough, the music press also struggled to place Badly Drawn Boy musically. Was he joining the new wave of anti-folk singers, in the vein of American prospects like The Moldy Peaches and Regina Spektor? Or was there a more traditional singer-songwriter hiding under all the wool and whiskers? Nevertheless, hype quickly built around Gough, with word of a 'British Beck' beginning to circulate.

He signed to XL in 1999 (while also remaining a Twisted Nerve artist) and, having been given a major-label-sized budget, began recording material for his debut record in peripatetic style. During the sessions, most of which took place at Gough's own studio, he seemingly worked with most of Manchester's available musicians, including all members of Doves, Martin Rebelski, and his Twisted Nerve label-mates Alfie and Mum & Dad. On production, Ken Nelson – who also worked with Coldplay on *Parachutes* later that year – Gary Wilkinson, Joe Robinson and Votel himself all took shifts; different producers are even credited for different sections of the same song. The sleeve lists a vast number of instruments too, including clavichord, vibraphone, horns, theremin, not to mention a vast array of samples and found sounds. All the signs pointed to Gough's debut album being a longer, messier version of his inscrutably pretty EPs. Yet when the hour arrived, it proved a very different beast indeed.

An 18-track exercise in both patient world-building and classic songwriting, *The Hour of Bewilderbeast* still sounds astoundingly fresh at twenty years' remove. The cover artwork, orchestrated by Votel and modelled on Leonardo da Vinci's *Vitruvian Man*, is playfully suggestive of the library of keepsakes contained in all of us: a circular, multi-compartmental shelf which houses a bevy of trinkets, fairy lights, mementoes and other assorted whatnots, all arranged in the rough shape of a figure. For a teenager increasingly preoccupied with the complexity of inner existence, the fallibility of the human body, and the realities of romantic love, it became a totemic image.

'The Shining', which opens the album with its golden, Christmassy brass section and see-sawing cello, apart from being an immediately moving piece of music, also represented a serious declaration: the Boy had matured. Gone, for the most part, were the intentional studio mishaps and gloopy production; *Bewilderbeast* was a fully-realised and forensically considered body of work. As the album's title would suggest, this is music to be listened to in one full sitting. Each track has been weighed up and set down precisely where it is to complement those around it. Gough describes it as 'a song cycle, really. The first song, in a metaphorical way, describes meeting [long-term partner] Claire, and I was writing that album in the early stages of our relationship.'[41] Even apparently throwaway instrumentals like

[41] Claire added backing vocals to *Bewilderbeast*'s closing track 'Epitaph', despite being an extremely reluctant vocalist. Reminiscing on Twitter, Gough reports that she needed 'a bottle of wine for courage!'

'Bewilder', essentially an organ-led prelude to the longer instrumental 'Bewilderbeast', do much to add texture and depth to the collection, and are not to be skipped. The sequencing of what Votel calls the 'water suite' ('Fall in a River', 'Camping Next to Water', 'Stone on the Water' and 'Another Pearl') provides a narrative swell in an album which brims with subplots and meanders. 'Camping Next to Water' is particularly noteworthy as a miniature tale of duty, favour and regret. You can almost see the protagonist's condensed breath drifting over the frost-covered banks. And if *The Hour of Bewilderbeast* is an attempt to chart a whole relationship in sixty minutes, the centre should promise something dangerously close to transcendence; 'Once Around the Block', with its buoyant kite-string melody and sighing doo-wop background vocals, delivers it.

The second half of *Bewilderbeast* steers us into territory closer to Gough's early work. 'This Song' is a wobbly ninety-second wonder; 'Cause a Rockslide' sounds like T-Rex in a stairwell. Yet there is pop savvy here, too. 'Pissing in the Wind' (re-recorded with the more radio-friendly 'spitting' for its single release) is one of the most straightforward songs on the album, but it shines amidst the more discursive numbers. And then, as if to prove he really *can* do anything, Gough throws in a crisp disco number in the shape of the magnificent 'Disillusion', which also features members of Doves. 'Please don't leave me wanting more', pleads the chorus of the closer, 'Epitaph'.[42] We don't need to ask for more after such a rich and varied hour; whether by accident or more likely by design, Gough had crafted a masterpiece. For me, it became another album to hide in.

Bewilderbeast won critical acclaim from all corners. *Pitchfork*, amazed by the disparity between live shambles and recorded brilliance celebrated it as 'a concise tour through the gentler side of British songwriting history – from understated psychedelia to sylvan protest folk'. In a review that reads pleasingly like a school report, *AllMusic* wrote 'Despite all attempts to sabotage his songwriting ... Damon Gough has to face the fact that he wrote and produced over a dozen excellent songs of baroque folk-pop.' The *NME* also commented on *Bewilderbeast*'s 'unambiguously cohesive' nature in their slightly more

---

[42] 'Epitaph' uses a tuning shown to Gough by Erlend Øye of Kings of Convenience. The Kings were fixtures of the Manchester scene during their time in England; more on them later.

hesitant 7/10 review. Though undeniably lifted by such encouraging feedback, it's unlikely that Gough or Votel could possibly have hoped *Bewilderbeast* would win the Mercury Prize that year. Collecting his cheque and trophy from the previous winner, Talvin Singh, Gough asks him 'What's your year been like? About the same?' He then thanks fellow nominees Coldplay, who 'never shut up about me, God bless them', and his close friends and collaborators, Doves. He then encourages the audience in the room and at home to buy the other shortlisted albums, as well as his own. In a post-speech interview with Jo Whiley he admits to 'shaking like a leaf' – still a picture of incomprehension at his achievement. 'Good things don't happen to good people, normally,' he says. And though the victory felt like a good thing at the time, it propelled Gough very quickly to heights he was arguably unprepared for.

For the moment, though, it seemed things were going swimmingly. Badly Drawn Boy's next record, the soundtrack to the Hugh Grant-starring adaptation of Nick Hornby's *About a Boy* (2002), was an unexpected yet genuinely charming proposition. Although it was greeted with surprise at the time, in retrospect, it made sense: *The Hour of Bewilderbeast* had been soundtrack-like in its construction too, its use of interludes and recurring motifs suggesting Gough was more of a traditional composer than even he might have imagined. Soundtrack work also provided a neat solution to the 'difficult second album' problem; he describes being freed from 'the burden of simply representing myself. It is a nice rewarding feeling … a liberating way of making music, so whilst there might not be a vast difference in results, the process is a little bit easier in terms of the stress that it puts on me. I wish that I could apply that more to my own writing.' Gough smoothed some of the rougher sonic edges found on *Bewilderbeast,* luxuriating instead in the gloss provided by the London Metropolitan Orchestra. That refinement is evident throughout the record, but it reaches a peak on the exquisitely-produced 'I Love NYE', which transfigures the chord structure of affable single 'Something to Talk About' into something approaching high art: a luminous, genuinely affecting orchestral suite. Elsewhere, Lennon-esque flights of fancy such as 'Silent Sigh' and 'File Me Away' mingle with lithe, fleet-footed constructions like 'Above You, Below Me' and 'River, Sea, Ocean'. There's even a heartfelt Christmas song in the shape of 'Donna and Blitzen', and when a wide-eyed Gough sings 'we're gonna see things we've never believed', one almost turns a discreet eye upwards, scanning the sky for a flash of antler. Gough's ventriloquising of the film's characters is also impressive, channelling the narcissism of Hugh Grant's character – the one-hit-wonder Christmas songwriter, Will – with a lightness of touch that many stage writers would envy. And it was surely no coincidence that, in several scenes, Nicholas Hoult's character, Marcus (the titular boy), wears headgear not dissimilar to Gough's own. Along with such a wholesome, mainstream project came further acceptance; a sense that Gough had quickly become part of the furniture of English culture. In three short years, he had gone from a beanie-sporting lo-fi songwriter, to... well, a beanie-sporting *hi*-fi songwriter. Except now your mum knew who he was. And though *About a Boy* was a conceptual and commercial triumph for Badly Drawn Boy (hitting number six in the charts, his highest album placing to date), there was a lingering sense among critics and fans that Gough had strayed too far into twee territory. His next album *Have You Fed the Fish?*[43] – written in Los Angeles at the same time as *About a Boy,* and also released in 2002 – found Gough attempting to reconcile the two sides of his songwriting, and to express bewilderment at his own rapid rise to fame. ('I'm turning Madonna down', he sings, memorably, on 'You Were Right'.) The result was a slight imbalance: untethered from a unifying theme or set of characters to draw from, *Have You Fed the Fish?* sounded unfocused. Nevertheless, the excellent singles 'You Were Right', 'All Possibilities' and 'Born Again' all charted respectably, and the album scored Gough another Top Ten.[44] There were also moments where romantic tenderness cut through the expansive arrangements: 'I Was Wrong' ironically stands out for its simplicity, a pleasingly downbeat miniature which morphs neatly into 'You Were Right'. But the album's real highlight – and one of Gough's very finest songs – is 'How?', a multi-tiered creation which

[43] The title inspired by the question he would ask his partner Claire every day on his phone calls home.
[44] All but one of Badly Drawn Boy's records have made the Top Twenty – quite the feat for an artist perennially viewed as an outsider.

shapeshifts from acoustic ditty, to showtune, to driving new wave and back again, all in the space of four minutes – illustrating just how high the Boy was aiming at this point. 'How?' also gave voice to the existential questions increasingly playing on Gough's mind. 'I tended to come out with questions about what this job entails for me – the amount of travelling I do, the time away from home … Talking with people on the street, they expect something of you, to add something to their lives … I've got a line, "How can I give you the answers you need, when all I possess is a melody?"'

Gough toured the album extensively in America, presumably mainlining a lot of his hero Bruce Springsteen's work in the process.[45] Yet even as he began to embrace the idea of rock stardom, he was missing his roots: reported homesickness saw him return to England, specifically Stockport, to record the quieter and more intimate *One Plus One is One* (2004). The sense that things had moved too far and too fast for Badly Drawn Boy was inescapable; *Bewilderbeast* remains both his finest achievement – and the work that continues to cast a shadow over the rest of his fine catalogue.

★★★

---

[45] Gough chose Springsteen as his specialist subject on *Celebrity Mastermind* in 2015.

Alfie were relative latecomers to this gifted Manchester microclimate. Though often positioned towards the front of the acoustic movement, they were far from traditional purveyors of indie-rock: instead, Alfie's was a shuffling, pleasantly elusive smorgasbord of folk, jazz and post-rock – far closer in outlook to the likes of Jim O'Rourke, Tortoise or Yo La Tengo than to any of their British contemporaries. Kitty Empire came closest to describing their sound in an early live review: 'Imagine the young Stone Roses infusing their laconic Manc cool into The Beta Band's meandering 21st-century folk.' Alfie singer and flame-keeper Lee Gorton reflects on the quality of the scene at the time:

> Everybody was good … we had a sense that something was going on. I mean, Elbow are Genesis-sized now – you've got be careful that you don't rewrite stuff. But they were clearly grander, and had a bigger scope. We were still too young, even, to know how amazing Madchester was. We all

knew someone with connections to it – but at the time you don't think, 'wow, that's incredible that the whole industry is looking here'. So when we were all coming through, we didn't really think about the future either.[46]

Alfie was initially the brainchild of Gorton and multi-instrumentalist Ian Smith, but the two always envisioned a bigger outfit:

It was always supposed to grow. I always liked to have as many people involved as possible – but I always wanted a core, a heart for it. I had a vision when I started putting it together, but that vision changed along the way. The truest qualities of it got truer. We didn't want to sound like anyone else in its finished version. Our influences got more disparate the more the lads' personalities came into the project – and I thought that was vital, that was great.

In that spirit, and to further bolster the band's live sound, Gorton recruited two music students, Matt McGeever (cello/guitar) and Sam Morris (bass), who began to add depth and musicality to Gorton and Smith's sketches. According to Andy Votel, he and the band first encountered each other as spectators watching the chaotic aftermath of a ram-raid robbery on Market Street: 'hordes of weekend revellers were helping themselves to stuffed toys'. The Alfie lads continued to show up on Votel's radar, and eventually won him over to their sound with the help of Clair Pearson from the band Mum & Dad, who were already on Twisted Nerve at this point. 'In hindsight they were a bit like the gang in *The Lost Boys*, in corduroy trousers … so they seemed like the perfect fit,' says Votel. It was a turning point in the Alfie story – not just for the opportunities a deal with Twisted Nerve promised, but also because of the serious musical education that came as part of Votel's friendship.

We had really esoteric tastes – for lads from Eccles – but when the Manchester scene opened up for us, that was wonderful. Andy Votel's record collection was wonderful – I've only ever heard a tiny part of it. We liked The Zombies and The Beach Boys and Elliott Smith – but we didn't know about The Left

[46] Author interview with Lee Gorton, October 2019. All subsequent quotes taken from this interview unless otherwise stated.

Banke and Jim O'Rourke and Broadcast … You can't really find the real lost gems without a bit of help.

The band quickly established themselves in what was now becoming a densely peopled scene, honing their own set while also continuing to provide backing for Gough at his live shows.

> It felt like a broad, creative family. Places like Night & Day, and the Roadhouse… we were very proud to be accepted into it. We had felt like the odd ones out – particularly compared to Elbow and Doves, who were all much more experienced, and closer to the finished article. Elbow had been going for 10 years already – we'd only been going for 10 minutes! Doves had already been Sub Sub, been on *Top of the Pops* … We were there among these bands, but we knew we were the most unlikely fit. We knew that what we were doing didn't make as much sense as those other bands.

If *Bewilderbeast* was a comforting snowglobe of an album, Alfie's first collection, released a year later in March 2001, was a melting ice cream to be savoured on a summer afternoon. In another move that drew comparisons with The Beta Band, this 'debut album' was in fact a compilation of the band's first three EPs released by Twisted Nerve at intervals throughout 2000 – though Gorton is more than happy to call it their first 'proper' record. The title, *If You Happy With You Need Do Nothing*, derives from a wonkily-worded letter Lee Gorton received from his dentist, but it quickly became a beloved phrase of the band.

> The sentence just sang to me. I don't think I would have called anything that now, but at the time we were so in the moment, we just thought 'that's it, that's great'. We were fearless – we didn't stop and think 'Is that really a snappy title…?' I really love the sentiment of it. There's a kind of Daoist simplicity to it.

That playfulness is also reflected in the aesthetics of Alfie. Just look at the artwork of *If You Happy With You Need Do Nothing*. The band's logo, spelt out in bubble-writing. The faded fabric landscape that adorns the front cover; the collage of photos and ephemera contained within the CD insert. Gorton even recalls asking producer Joe Robinson, 'Can you make it sound any more corduroy?'[47] It is all suggestive of a homemade era, of scratchy cardigans with elbow-patches, when Oliver Postgate's stop-motion creations roamed the land, wearing their old buttons like medals. It's an attitude that informed the band's choice of instruments, too, as Gorton remembers:

> It was just whatever we had – we were buying old synths whenever we saw them, I was working the markets at the time so I would buy anything. Bitty, ramshackle, slightly broken old Moogs and stuff. But it was kind of cute, and the lads could get a sound out of anything. The arrangements that Sam and Matt were coming up with, coupled with these tumbledown synths and shit, that's where it all came from.

For all its fuzzy edges, however, *If You Happy With* is shot through with singles of remarkable clarity and quality. Strings bow and creak gracefully around opener 'Bookends', Gorton's dazed exhortations entering the arrangement like a drowsy wasp circling a pint of cider. Gorton quipped in an interview with *Free Williamsburg* in 2002, 'None of us are doing this because we are great singers. None of us are great poets really … We are just trying to catch the vibe of the music. The music always comes first.' Accordingly, Joe Robinson nestles the lead vocals low in the mix, not giving prominence to any element over another, a kind of egalitarian production. This has a double effect: it helps the listener to imagine Alfie as a single, cohesive unit, while also inviting them to lean in and pay closer attention. It's the same intimacy that flowed through *Bewilderbeast* and even *White Ladder* – a quality which had been desperately lacking for much of the previous decade. The rain-dodging chorus of 'It's Just About the Weather' is another bucolic wonder, and a further addition to the apparent slew of meteorological hits being released at the time. The instrumental 'James's Dream' serves as an early interlude, leaving a breadcrumb trail of plucked melody and half-remembered conversations. And then comes 'You Make No Bones', a bouncy and

---

[47] 'Ha, yeah I remember that,' says Gorton. 'It feels so stupid to have said that now. It's one of those things that, 10 years ago, you'd be kicking yourself for, but… it's sort of sweet in its naivety.'

hummable single which is also the song in which Gorton's vocals most closely resemble Ian Brown's – or perhaps more pertinently, Liam Gallagher's.

It's worth investigating those comparisons a little. Manchester's cultural dominance of the preceding decade had been imperious and overarching, and at the heart of it were three indomitable frontmen: Ian Brown, Liam Gallagher, and Sir Alex Ferguson.[48] Sadly, there isn't much recorded evidence of the latter's singing chops, but critics were understandably eager to seek out a new Brown or Gallagher; to find the next link in an already gilded artistic chain. They sensed they might be onto something with Gorton, who boasted both the impish good looks and the nonchalant vocal delivery required to be a contender. But his casual manner was deceptive. It wasn't a by-product of arrogance, but of a good-natured bonhomie – what Lee Gorton describes in the *Free Williamsburg* interview as 'a band at ease with itself'. Alfie simply weren't fussed with swagger. They were more interesting than that.

> I guess there was a little bit of [comparison to Brown/ Gallagher] – you can't deny it, I've got a strong northern accent, and I'm not that great a singer – I know that … The other lads could all sing in tune better than me. I didn't even know what a harmony was when we started the band – I still don't really know how they work. But yes, if you look across the spectrum of singers, I'm much closer to Ian Brown than Nina Simone, aren't I?

Almost as if testing listeners tempted by the lure of a new Roses or Oasis, the second half of *If You Happy With* invites them down some less well-trodden paths. 'Umlaut's toppling chorus; 'Check the Weight's drum'n'brass outro, which leaves the impression of a tipsy oompah band tottering into the distance; the tender vocal harmonies of 'Manor House Farm', which contest Gorton's insistence they weren't the band's strong point. And what better way to end this most horizontal of records than with 'Montevideo', its most languid

---

[48] Ferguson's tenure as manager of Manchester United peaked on 27th May 1999, as his team paraded an unprecedented (and, at time of writing, unrepeated) treble of Premier League, FA Cup and UEFA Champions League trophies through the city.

cut? *If You Happy With* was a British summer of an album: sweet, unpredictable, a little strange – and over too soon.

Critics were seduced by Alfie's sound, with Victoria Segal's *NME* review particularly complimentary. She also highlights the pitfalls of making a slow and quiet album in the era of acoustic and 'chillout', praising the band for mostly avoiding them. '[T]his is music that is far from naïve or innocent – there should be no doubt that we are dealing with a smart band here … we certainly happy with, for now.' In a *Drowned in Sound* review that also dismisses the New Acoustic Movement as 'this most puritan, regressive of musical dog tags' – another indicator of the instant backlash it was subject to – Tom Eyers praises Alfie for standing apart from it: 'a refreshing alternative to a somewhat turgid homegrown music scene'. Despite the mostly positive reception for *If You Happy With*, the lack of a big single meant that it didn't unduly bother the charts, entering the Top 100 at number 62 in April 2001, and lasting just one week there. There must have been a slight sense of deflation for the band, given the major-prize-winning achievements of their label-mate Damon Gough. Alfie were experiencing the perks and pitfalls of working with a small independent: the band had retained and increased their credibility; but Twisted Nerve were never going to have the marketing clout of a major. Gorton began to feel restless.

The songs from *If You Happy With* were in some cases several years old, so Alfie were able to follow up their debut quickly with newer compositions. The result was *A Word in Your Ear* (2002). Another slice of rustic beauty, it boasted a useful crop of singles, including 'Cloudy Lemonade' and 'Bends for 72 Miles'. Yet the recording of the album was partially overshadowed by an emergent awkwardness between Alfie and their label, with the band now keen to try their luck elsewhere but contracted to a second album with Twisted Nerve. However, it seems time has healed whatever wounds there were, and Gorton has reconciled any dispute:

> It was frustrating at the time, and maybe when you think about what could have been – but our connections at Twisted Nerve were wonderful for us. With the second album, because we already wanted out, we were foolishly saving things for the third album … if anything's regretful, it's that.

I dare say whatever we thought we were saving for *Do You Imagine Things?* didn't get on it anyway! I think *A Word in Your Ear* is probably my least favourite because of all that. It's a minor quibble, now. I'm really grateful for everything that we got to do with Twisted Nerve. I've made peace with everything else.

Having fulfilled their duties at Twisted Nerve, Alfie were signed by Parlophone, who had apparently been courting the band from as early as 1998, and recorded *Do You Imagine Things?* (2003) with Ken Nelson. Gorton's eyes light up when I mention the sessions, which were clearly a highlight of his time with the band. It's an enjoyment that shines through on every second of *Do You Imagine Things?*, Alfie's boldest and best album. Yet with a bigger label came increased pressure: following Coldplay's achievements in the same stable with *Parachutes* and *A Rush of Blood to the Head*, there was an unconscious drive to create something more commercial. It's an anxiety that informs 'People', 'our attempt at a hit', as Gorton says. Sadly, it wasn't quite hit enough, and Alfie's fourth album *Crying at Teatime* (2005) proved not to contain the big numbers required of them either. The band split later that year, with Gorton evidently frustrated with the lack of impact his hard work was having. He certainly sounds downcast in a report on the split from *Manchester Evening News*: 'Some of the band felt we weren't getting the breaks anymore. Not that you're owed them mind, but it's easy to lose heart when you've been trying to do things your own way for so long yet still not getting the response you're after.'

Gorton has subsequently stepped away from music; Alfie's delightfully intangible work lies waiting to be rediscovered.

3. The Students in the Stadium
Coldplay and Snow Patrol

Coldplay – *Parachutes*
Snow Patrol – *When It's All Over We Still Have To Clear Up*

As well as providing more than its fair share of local talent, Manchester also served as a proving ground for a plethora of young acts from across the land in the nineties and early noughties, thanks to the In The City showcases. Initially envisioned by Tony Wilson and his partner Yvette Livesey in 1992 as a platform for new and upcoming bands to mix with industry insiders and record companies, it quickly grew into an institution – a hotly contested gig with a reputation for breeding success. Inevitably, the conference also acted as a cultural barometer. Suede, Radiohead and Oasis graced 1992's event, and for the rest of the decade it played host every autumn to the brightest lights in the musical firmament. By 1998, as Britpop's stars dimmed, the In The City lineup was already anticipating the next wave, with two bands in particular dominating the stakes that year. The first was Muse, led by Matt Bellamy – who would achieve enormous success in the coming decade with their blend of astral paranoia and breathless, serpentine prog rock. The other? A band of four scruffy lads who'd come up from London for the day, looking like they'd just emerged from their student digs and picked up any instruments they happened to have to hand. (This was only half true.) They were the last band added to the convention's bill that year, and were almost totally unknown to the industry wags wandering the city that week. Nevertheless, when 'The Coldplay' took to the stage at Cuba Cafe – to an audience that some estimates don't even put into double figures – it represented the beginning of something truly extraordinary. In The City had built a solid reputation for uncovering the next big thing – now, it had found the biggest.

It's fair to say that the figures in this book are not the most immediately obvious pop stars. Their image, their music, and the values that come across in their interviews – humility, relatability and a certain take-it-or-leave-it attitude to wider recognition – all hardly augured fame and fortune. Yet many of them achieved it.

Coldplay are the most obvious example; *Parachutes* started them on a journey towards becoming one of the only global success stories from the period. They have also continued to thrive *after* it, outstripping even their earlier achievements. Snow Patrol – who entered a phase of similar dominance following the release of 2003's *Final Straw* – effectively warmed up for that record with 2001's *When It's All Over We Still Have To Clear Up*, which saw them begin to shake off their more eccentric indie trappings. Chris Martin admits 'Coldplay will never be cool' in a 2008 *Telegraph* interview, and the same could be said for Snow Patrol – but you suspect neither band cares. Having successfully made leaps from student nights into the mainstream, they now enjoy the kind of global success their peers could only dream of.

★★★

COLDPLAY · PARACHUTES

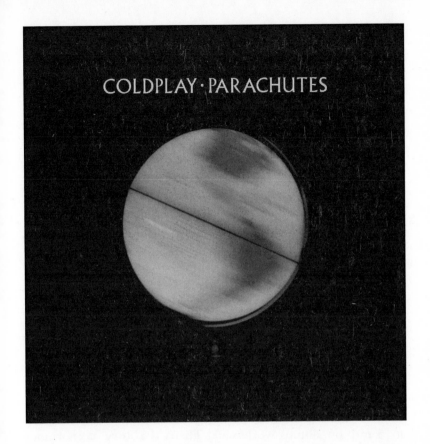

Glastonbury 2019 saw Chris Martin – Coldplay's effusive, somehow eternally youthful frontman – make two starkly different cameo appearances. Firstly, on the Friday evening, as the Pyramid Stage began to cool after a day of intense heat, Martin played a bit part in Stormzy's breathtaking, masterfully choreographed coronation of UK grime. Met with a roar from the gigantic crowd, he joined the MC on stage midway through the set, and they sat beside each other at a piano for a simple, intimate rendition of 'Blinded by Your Grace Pt.1'. As the song drifted out over the fields, it formed a moment of sultry solitude, a natural pause between eye-popping set-pieces. The duo shared a warm embrace, Martin threw the crowd his trademark sheepish wave, and he was gone. His second appearance that weekend was again on the Pyramid Stage, this time joining Kylie Minogue during Sunday's so-called 'Legend's Slot'. Greeted by a sun-drenched audience, Minogue and Martin teased their way through an acoustic version of 'Can't Get You Out of My Head'. Again, the Coldplay man provided levity in a visually spectacular show. And while his two appearances may have been mere walk-ons, the effect was clear: Coldplay, and Martin in particular, now transcended genre and demographic; they fitted everywhere. They have done for quite some time.

A quick rundown of Martin's collaborators and associates gives you an idea of Coldplay's extensive cultural reach, unmatched by any other 'traditional' band working today: Beyoncé, Jay-Z, Pharrell Williams, Avicii, Michael Stipe, Rihanna, The Flaming Lips… the list goes on. The range of artists is also important here: Coldplay are different, and more successful, because they can adapt at will. That doesn't make them sellouts; far from it. It makes them very, very good at their jobs. Coldplay's is a continuing musical rebirth; their willingness to collaborate and expand their sound beyond their core setup has proved crucial to their endurance. But in truth, the band's vision has been world-encompassing from the very beginning: the globe on the cover of their debut album, *Parachutes*, was an obvious clue.[49] That ambition saw them quickly shrug off their early status as critical whipping boys of the New Acoustic Movement, becoming one of the biggest-selling bands of all time: estimates put their sales at 75 million albums worldwide. Theirs is a story of enormous and consistent progress, driven forward by a frontman with an uncommon knack for crafting anthems on an epic scale. Not bad for an accountant's son from Exeter; or for a band whose earliest recordings came under the name 'Big Fat Noises'.

Guitarist Jonny Buckland, bassist Guy Berryman and Chris Martin met in September 1996, playing together while living in Ramsay Hall, a halls-of-residence linked to University College London, where they were all students. Chris and Jonny met first over a game of pool, and their musical connection was obvious from the outset. 'Meeting Jonny was like falling in love. He could make all the ideas work and we were writing two songs a night sometimes.' Guy joined shortly afterwards, and the trio began writing and rehearsing more seriously. Having perfected a number of songs in the first

[49] Bought from WH Smith for £10, the globe – as well as being a cover star – was for a time the band's sole stage prop, both at their early shows and during the *Parachutes* years.

half of 1997 (including the first 'official' Coldplay composition, 'Ode to Deodorant'), they decided to put together a demo for an *NME* Unsigned Showcase – but they were missing a drummer. The inexperienced but enthusiastic Will Champion completed the lineup in July, and they recorded the *Panic EP* under the Big Fat Noises moniker.

The band missed out on the showcase slot, but quickly found themselves playing shows in and around Camden anyway: renaming themselves to the barely-less-bad Starfish, their first public performance was at the Laurel Tree on 16th January 1998. The set list included 'High Speed' and 'Panic', versions of which would eventually make it on to their debut album. In the crowd that night was Phil Harvey, a friend of Martin's who regularly visited them from Oxford, where he was studying Classics. He expressed a wish to be more involved with the band, having put on student nights at college bars in the city, and, helping them out of a dispute with a local promoter in Camden later in the year, independently booked and promoted a well-attended show at Dingwalls.[50] From then on, he and Coldplay were inseparable – he is often referred to as the fifth member. Harvey was also instrumental in getting them on tape again, stumping up £1500 for the recording of their first official EP, *Safety,* which was self-released in February 1998 and limited to 500 copies – the majority of which were sent out to record companies, DJs and other industry types.[51] It was their first release under the name 'Coldplay' – although the band would toy with an added 'The' for a while afterwards. (The name derives from the title of a poetry collection by Philip Horky, *Child's Reflections, Cold Play*). The effect of *Safety* remains striking: although far from the finished article, 'Bigger Stronger', 'No More Keeping My Feet on the Ground' and 'Such a Rush' formed the blueprint for everything to come.

[50] They also played two shows that summer at Guttridge's Yard in Stoke Newington alongside a band called 'Cherry Keane' – later known as Keane. Tim Rice-Oxley, the band's keyboardist and songwriter, became great friends with Chris Martin, and the two bands were supportive of each other as they established themselves. Keane took a little longer to break through, but their debut album *Hopes and Fears* (2004) went straight to number one, and the band now find themselves categorised alongside Coldplay and Snow Patrol as part of the acoustic movement – despite famously eschewing guitars.

[51] During Coldplay's first Evening Session on Radio 1, Steve Lamacq admits that *Safety* 'completely passed me by'. Martin playfully responds, 'But we put a copy in your pigeonhole... You didn't listen to it, you bastard!' (*Going Deaf for a Living.*)

Then came a lucky break. With some of their members working as part-time cleaners over the summer, 'The' Coldplay (as they were named that week) were granted a somewhat last-minute place at 1998's edition of the In The City convention in Manchester, playing on 14th September at Cuba Cafe on Port Street. Debs Wild – who is credited as the first music industry bod to set eyes on the band, and now acts as their fan liaison – was then working as a scout for Universal. She recalls being one of just a handful of people in the audience:

> That year was a good year for In The City. Elbow were there, Muse, a band called Younger Younger 28s … Cay, a great dirty grunge band whose singer is no longer with us. I saw 50 of the 54 bands in the programme – and it would have been the full 54 if it hadn't been for Coldplay being so good, because I couldn't leave their set, I wanted to see it all. People used to ask me 'What are you looking for?' and I'd say 'I don't know, but I'll know when I see it', and that was the first time in a really big way that I thought 'this is that feeling'.[52]

Steve Lamacq describes a similar sensation upon seeing the band for the first time at the Camden Falcon later that year:

> I go to a lot of gigs. But it's very rare at the bottom level that you see a band who are 'ready' … you see bands who are excitable and nervous and all the more charming for it; and you see bands who will go on to be popular in nine months or a year's time. You hardly ever see a band that is 'ready'. But Coldplay were ready.

The band's musical promise was clearly abundant, although at this stage there was little to suggest the forensic attention to detail that would eventually define Coldplay's visuals. As Wild puts it:

> They looked dreadful. I can't put it any other way, they looked really bad. They didn't have a cohesive sense of style, it was just four random people on a stage. They didn't look like

[52] Author interview with Debs Wild, October 2019.

they'd thought about that at all, which was ironic because now they think about it a heck of a lot. So yes, they weren't style over substance, put it that way!

Coldplay's apparent apathy towards fashion was typical of the bands who broke through at the time. Britpop had been closely aligned with the sartorial trends of the nineties; think of the flashy sportswear favoured by Blur and Oasis, or the fitted formals of Pulp and Suede. In contrast, barely any of the acoustic bands had a coherent look to speak of. Perhaps this indifference stemmed from the fact that everything Britpop-related – including the fashion – was fast on its way out, with no new trend yet to establish itself. Again, the everyman appeal came to the fore: here were future pop stars who looked and dressed just like we did.

The band continued to play around the country and appeared on Lamacq's Radio 1 Evening Session on 25th February 1999. With record companies continuing to court them, they released 'Brothers and Sisters' as a one-off single on Fierce Panda that April. Debs Wild lobbied hard to get Coldplay over to Universal; in the end, they signed with Parlophone, after scout Dan Keeling had taken a particular shine to 'No More Keeping My Feet on the Ground'. The summer of 1999 must have felt particularly sweet, as the band all graduated with respectable degrees and secured a record deal into the bargain (bizarrely, the contract was signed on a trestle table that Keeling had erected in Trafalgar Square). With major-label backing, the band now readied themselves as best they could to record their debut album – unfortunately, it would take longer than Coldplay or Parlophone envisioned. They began the sessions with Beta Band producer Chris Allison, but the atmosphere quickly turned fraught; the band came apart at the seams, spooked by the pressure of performing at such a high level. They even briefly jettisoned Will Champion, auditioning several other drummers before realising his presence was needed and welcoming him back. Allison departed the Coldplay project instead, and after the band recorded 'Bigger Stronger' and 'Such a Rush' in July 1999 themselves, the resulting patchwork was released as an EP, *The Blue Room*, that October. Fazed by the experience, Coldplay returned to gigging and rehearsal while they sought another producer; 'High Speed' was the only track from the Allison sessions to make it on to *Parachutes*.

Martin's increasingly powerful falsetto and Buckland's mellifluous guitar lines inevitably earned them early comparisons to Radiohead. And though there were undeniable similarities, Coldplay never shared Yorke and co.'s political paranoia, nor their avant-garde tendencies. Not that they particularly needed to. Coldplay's power was clearly in their ability to weave memorable melodies from even the sparsest of arrangements. 'See You Soon' – a fixture of their set for many years – was an especially fine example from *The Blue Room*. Listen again to Buckland's guitar part: intimate, crepuscular, a world away from the skyscraping chimes of later tracks like 'In My Place'. His fingers dart audibly over the strings, stoking that front-room feeling. And Martin's vocals, while not necessarily invested with the clarity they would achieve on later records, are beautifully tender. 'See You Soon' was an elegant line drawing, a precursor to the pyrotechnic splatters that lay ahead. The band's next phase saw them add more colours to the palette – and one in particular was about to make their name.

Ken Nelson, who had just completed work on his sections of *The Hour of Bewilderbeast*, was drafted in for the new Coldplay sessions in November 1999. They took place at Parr Street in Liverpool, Rockfield Studios in Monmouthshire, and Wessex Studios in London. The Rockfield sessions would prove especially fruitful, yielding 'Shiver' and 'Don't Panic', but also providing a crucial slice of inspiration. On a particularly clear evening, the splendour of the rural night sky drew band and producer outside. The stars seemed to be shining for them. Martin began writing what he thought was an off-the-cuff ditty, complete with a hokey Neil Young impression, to make the rest of the band laugh. He'd actually just written the song that would catapult them to success.

'Yellow' is now a song so ubiquitous it feels almost futile to write about it. I heard it on the radio many, many times, and bought it on the day it was released: 26th June 2000. It's lucky that CDs are more durable than vinyl, because I played that single to *death*. But then, so did everyone else. 'Yellow' reached number four in the charts, and it stayed in the Top 100 for the best part of six months. It represented an enormous and unexpected breakthrough for Coldplay; 'Shiver' had only reached number 35. As well as its admirable chart performance, 'Yellow' seemed to cast an enduring spell over the British public, resonating in the same way that 'Why Does It Always Rain On Me?' had done a year earlier for Travis. It was a song whose genius lay in its simplicity. When you really get down to it, not many people can remember *every single word* of that many songs; what Chris Martin seems to have realised early on is that the key to catchiness is economy. 'Yellow' is a perfect example: after you discount the repetitions within the verses, chorus and coda, its vocabulary is just over fifty words. It's a technique Coldplay still use to this day – and one they would road-test fully on their debut album.

If you've picked up this book, I reckon the chances are you still listen to *Parachutes* on a regular basis, just as I do. And why not? Whatever your thoughts on Coldplay's cultural standing now, there's no disputing its power, potency and beauty. Yet beneath the surface, things were not so pristine for Coldplay. The album's troubled genesis is well documented, as the perfectionism, self-doubt and paranoia that had emerged during the *Blue Room* sessions returned with a vengeance – qualities which would intermittently plague the band's writing and recording process for the next two decades. In a *Select* interview from 2001, the band recalls the uneasy studio atmosphere:

> 'We sweated over it, argued over it, went through a lot of unhappiness and pain,' says Chris. 'We were reeling from it for quite a bit.'
>
> Even Jonny Buckland, a man who would probably greet news of impending nuclear holocaust with a nonchalant shrug, admits, 'The recording sessions were horribly tense. We thought it could be the last record we ever made so we might as well put everything into it. That's why we got so fraught – no second chances.'

Certainly 'Don't Panic' – perhaps an instruction to themselves? – is an unusual introduction to the band. At just over two minutes long, it feels more like a miniature portrait of Coldplay than it does a bold opening number, and you could argue its main purpose is to showcase Jonny Buckland's deliciously supple guitar voice. For the reclusive Buckland is the hidden weapon on *Parachutes*, channelling

Johnny Marr, The Edge and John Squire, but also harnessing a tone and temper all his own. Buckland has the rare gift of making his guitar sound as expressive and varied as a vocal line; he remains a consistently underrated guitarist despite his band's enormous profile. Buckland's playing also drives the muscular 'Shiver', which sees Chris Martin's voice truly soar for the first time on *Parachutes*. 'Shiver' is the heaviest track on the album, especially in its final section, where Buckland cuts loose. Although hardly a surprise to anyone with a pair of ears, Martin revealed the song's inspiration in a Radio 1 interview with Chris Moyles in 2008: 'It's a blatant Jeff Buckley attempt. Not quite as good, that's what I think. We were 21 and he was very much a hero, and as with those things it tends to filter through.' Heard in isolation, you wouldn't think it was the signature track of a band about to become key players in an acoustic revolution – it's actually closer in execution to their contemporaries, Muse. Both bands would attempt the galactic with their later efforts.

Further into *Parachutes* there are moments of relative calm. There's 'Sparks', with its closing-time bassline; and 'We Never Change', with its whispered percussion and careworn vocals. Even the album's title track, so often a defining statement for new bands, is a pretty and unassuming fragment of just under a minute. It's the kind of risk you feel the explosive latter-day Coldplay would hardly recognise, let alone consider releasing. And there's another interesting miniature hidden away at the end: running on after the gospel influenced 'Everything's Not Lost' is the beautiful 'Life is for Living', which clocks in at just over 90 seconds. The juxtaposition of these two starkly different songs made clear the musical directions the band found themselves pulled in – the acoustic, organic closeness of one, up against the soaring, lighters-aloft coda of the other. In Coldplay's case, there was only going to be one winner, and another of the album's key tracks, 'Trouble', provided a neat stepping-stone to the arenas they coveted. On it, Martin weaves from his piano the kind of circular, nagging melody he would go on to perfect on 'Clocks' and 'A Sky Full of Stars'.[53] 'Trouble' was the boldest instance thus far of Coldplay putting a piano at a song's core. It wouldn't be the last.

[53] Astonishingly only their second number one single (at time of writing).

Parachutes took even Parlophone by surprise with its instantaneous ascent. Debs Wild, who maintained a close connection with the band despite their decision to sign with a rival major, recalls the day its first-week chart placement was announced: 'The expectations for *Parachutes* were really low – I think everybody had a figure in their heads of "oh if it does this many then we'll be happy" – and it did that in its first week. Sitting on Primrose Hill with a bottle of champagne on the day of the charts, listening to the countdown on a little transistor radio, and then hearing that *Parachutes* was number one ... that was when I thought, "Okay, this is big."' She was not mistaken. On its initial release *Parachutes* spent nearly 18 unbroken months in the Top 100; since then, the album has spent a cumulative total of nearly four years on the chart. By the end of 2000, *Parachutes* had sold almost a million copies. It was a life-changing record.

Coldplay selected 'Trouble' as the third and final cut from the album, although 'Don't Panic' was also released as a non-UK single.[54] It reached number ten in the charts, proving 'Yellow' had not been a one-hit wonder. Yet as the sales of *Parachutes* continued to grow, and the award wins stacked up, there was a backlash simmering against this new wave of acoustic or otherwise polite music – with Coldplay bearing the brunt. Although *Parachutes* had gathered largely positive reviews from the music press, the Alan McGee outburst typified a feeling from more 'authentic' corners of the industry that, in contrast to the edgy nineties, the band were playing their hand too straight; were trying too hard; were simply not weird enough to be cool. 'There's something undeniably irritating about a band who try quite so hard to be ordinary,' wrote Victoria Segal in a gig review for *NME*. A 5.3 *Pitchfork* review of *Parachutes* typified the arch response from the hipper music press: 'Pretty, lovely, fine, fair, comely, pleasant, agreeable, acceptable, adequate, satisfactory, nice, benign, harmless, innocuous, innocent, largely unobjectionable, safe, forgettable.' As Martin recounts, again in the 2001 *Select* interview:

> I feel a bit like we're human cannonballs ... We've just been
> fired and while half the time you think, 'This is great we're

---

[54] The 'Don't Panic' single also featured a live cover version of the Bond theme 'You Only Live Twice', which had, by this point, become a regular addition to their setlist.

flying through the air', the other time you think, 'Shit, when are we going to land?' People who don't like you talk about you like you're the Third Reich. People who do like you will really defend you. So it's a mixture of extreme excitement and extreme, er, panic.

That panic inevitably hit Martin hardest, tapping into his insecurities about not being authentic enough. 'We're starting to feel that everyone's out to get us,' he told *Melody Maker* at the end of 2000. He also worried that as the band were, in honesty, all nice middle-class boys, they weren't offering the true rock'n'roll experience to their fans. A non-smoker and only very occasional drinker, in an interview with the *Observer* he admits to feeling inferior compared to 'real' rock stars like Liam Gallagher. Of course, that ordinariness was key to Coldplay's appeal; as their detractors continued to bleat away, the band's profile was only getting bigger. They toured the world in support of *Parachutes* for much of 2001, including dates in the US and Australasia, and sales of the album now surpassed five million. By October, the band were slated to begin recording their next album, but there was a problem – the songs had started to dry up. In an attempt to locate their mojo again, Chris dusted off a half-finished track from the *Parachutes* sessions, written on an old pump organ, called 'In My Place'. The song proved a catalyst for more, and soon the band were up to full speed again, heading to Parr Street with Ken Nelson to hunker down and finish what would become *A Rush of Blood to the Head*. Whilst there, further inspiration struck, with 'Daylight', 'A Whisper' and 'The Scientist' written during their six-week tenure. In an unlikely twist, Echo & The Bunnymen frontman Ian McCulloch also helped the band during the sessions – one of the few outsiders privy to the album's making. Coldplay were great admirers of McCulloch's band, and their cover of 'Lips Like Sugar' was a fixture in their set.[55] It also seems that McCulloch was pivotal in helping Martin overcome his self-doubt – by the following year, Coldplay were a very different prospect.

A Rush of Blood to the Head was released in August 2002, with the band premiering tracks from it on their website in the week running

---

[55] The band used a live version of the track as a B-side to 'God Put A Smile Upon Your Face'.

up to its appearance in shops. As if to draw a line under the *Parachutes* era, 'In My Place' outperformed 'Yellow' in the charts,[56] and both single and album were wrapped in serious, enigmatic artwork: a digitally altered head on a stark white background. It was a far cry from the fuzzy flower that adorned the cover of their best-known single.[57] Again making a Radiohead comparison in their assessment, *NME* acknowledged that '[*A Rush of Blood's*] closest relative is Radiohead's *The Bends*, the album that secured the notion that Radiohead had more in their locker than "Creep". Coldplay similarly needed to put "Yellow" to bed.' With *A Rush of Blood* they managed just that, and in some style. The collection makes its intentions plain from the very start: this is an unfettered leap for superstardom, with Chris Martin clearly emerging as the band's leader. Where 'Don't Panic' had served as something of a warm-up on *Parachutes*, there is no such hesitancy here. 'Politik', with its hammering piano and existential musings ('Look at Earth from outer space…') confirmed that, lyrically, we were no longer confined to the walls inside Martin's head.

The same shattering global events that spurred Travis on to make *12 Memories* also informed Coldplay's decision to attempt something vast in its scale, and millennial in its worries; it's no surprise to learn that 'Politik' was written on 13th September 2001. Consider the perspective suggested by that first line: instead of the 'beautiful world' of their first album, this was Earth viewed as a

[56] 'In My Place' was beaten to the number one spot in August 2002 by 'Colourblind', the debut single by *Popstars* and *Pop Idol* star Darius Danesh-Campbell. The story was presented at the time as a battle between 'manufactured' and 'authentic' music – a conversation that would dominate the decade as Simon Cowell's creations continued to sweep all before them. However, as Alex Petridis notes in his *Guardian* piece on the rise of 'boring pop', 'In truth, [Coldplay and Darius] had more in common than the adversarial narrative suggested.' The two would appear alongside each other on *NME's 1 Love* compilation, released later in 2002. The album is a curious but instructive snapshot of the era: a collection of cover versions of famous number ones by contemporary artists. Many of our acoustic heroes appear: Dido and Faithless cover Beats International's 'Dub Be Good to Me' and Starsailor bash through The Small Faces' 'All Or Nothing' – but the real highlight is Elbow's version of Thunderclap Newman's 'Something In The Air'; a version which comes close to bettering the original.
[57] This most distinctive of cover images actually came about as a result of a technological mishap. In a 2008 interview with *The Guardian*, photographer Sølve Sundsbø recalls being commissioned by *Dazed and Confused* to create images with a 'technological feel'. He experimented using a model and a 3D scanner, but the machine failed to pick up certain elements of his picture, rendering them as spikes instead; the top of the head was also cut off. As it turned out, *Dazed* loved the resulting portfolio – as did Chris Martin, who contacted him and asked if Coldplay could use them. Sundsbø recreated the process for the *A Rush of Blood* single artwork, this time using the band members as his subject.

small, insignificant part of something much bigger; realisations that would form the backbone of the album. Countless rock bands had covered this ground before – most recently The Verve, on their beatific 1997 masterpiece *Urban Hymns* – yet this was not the album of calculated commercial rock that its broad themes might suggest. Think of 'Green Eyes', a simple love song with a sweet country-rock tinge; 'Warning Sign' with its gently undulating guitars and touching chorus; 'The Scientist's plaintive assertions. *A Rush of Blood* was crammed with the warm humanity that had drawn so many to *Parachutes* – Coldplay were simply using a bigger canvas now, marrying planet-sized fears to the most secluded affairs of the heart. But it was another single, again with a looping piano riff at its heart, that was to prove the album's most enduring. Originally demoed too late for the *A Rush of Blood* sessions, which wrapped early in 2002, the song that became 'Clocks' was stashed on a tape marked 'Songs for #3' – referring to the band's third album. Yet according to an *Independent* piece in 2008, the song was 'the grit in the oyster', and with the band unsatisfied with the album as it stood (Chris Martin describes it in the same article as 'sounding rubbish') they delayed it, giving them time to revisit the song. Martin's instincts proved correct, and it won Record of the Year at the 2004 Grammys. The band's new-found confidence, especially when measured against the occasional hesitancy of *Parachutes*, is perhaps most evident on closing ballad 'Amsterdam'. Elements are added slowly and steadily, so that in the final two minutes, when the rest of the band crashes in, it registers not as a jolt, but as a logical conclusion. And if that makes it sound a little joyless, it shouldn't: there's a thrill in hearing a band controlling their sound so confidently. They were transforming before our eyes.

A Rush of Blood to the Head hit the sweet spot of critical appreciation and public adoration,[58] with critics gobsmacked at the change in Coldplay in such a short space of time. *The Times* caught the general mood of the press with its verdict: 'Where *Parachutes* was a tentative effort sprinkled with beauty, *A Rush of Blood to the Head* is expansive, adventurous and bulging with terrific songs.' The album went straight to number one and stayed there for three weeks – then, perhaps even

---

[58] What's more, its reputation has endured: in 2013, Radio 2 listeners voted it the greatest album of all time.

more impressively, it didn't leave the Top 100 for almost two years. 'The Scientist', then 'Clocks', joined 'In My Place' as Top Ten singles. In a dizzyingly short space of time, Coldplay had made the leap to megastardom that others craved, establishing themselves as the era's leading guitar band. Crucially they had, by this point, extracted themselves from any notion of acoustic leanings; by consciously uncoupling from fads like the New Acoustic Movement, or indeed any genre in particular, they could create and collaborate freely – thus ensuring their own continued success. As Buckland said of the *Rush of Blood* sessions: 'We didn't have to do the acoustic thing, we didn't have to do a loud rock thing, we didn't have to react against anything.' Much like their heroes, U2, Coldplay seemed to be a band always destined to play the biggest venues, to the biggest crowds – they just needed people to catch up with them. *Parachutes*, then, was Coldplay's equivalent to *Boy*: a fully formed debut, but one that positively crackled with grander intentions. Yet in comparison to the colossal scale of Coldplay's later work, *Parachutes* now feels modest, and perhaps therein lies the reason for its enduring appeal.

Reckoning with Coldplay's legacy is difficult because it is still so demonstrably alive, and Chris Martin will be gracing the biggest stages for many years to come. Theirs was a global vision from the outset, as Debs Wild reflects, 'Chris had a plan, and I think this was his destiny – I'm not even that spiritual, but I do feel it was that simple, it would have happened with or without me. We didn't have a crystal ball – we couldn't have known, but I just had a feeling I was watching something special.'

That specialness is augmented by Coldplay's practicality. Time and again, they have sensed the direction of music culture and written themselves into it; have been available and open-minded in their collaborations and experiments. For fans of the band who have been with them from the start, there will always be a special place for *Parachutes* – and there are still factions of their fanbase who long for the return of the 'old' Coldplay. They may attract derision for their perceived embrace of commercialism, or their lack of indie credentials, but even now, as the band celebrates 20 years since *Parachutes*'s release, there is something beguiling about their puppyish zeal for the new.

★★★

*snowpatrol

when it's all over we still have to clear up

In July 2019, an interesting statistic came to light. According to data from the music licensing company PPL, the most-played song on UK radio of the century so far was not a pop song, or a hip-hop song, as one might expect from the prevailing trends of the past two decades: it was 'Chasing Cars' by Snow Patrol. Taken from the band's 2006 album *Eyes Open*, the song had only reached number six in the UK charts, but it became ubiquitous, helped considerably by its appearances at key moments on the hit US medical drama *Grey's Anatomy*, including the season two finale. During that period, it also reached number five on the US Billboard charts, still rarefied territory for many UK artists. It had seemed like 'Chasing Cars' was inescapable at the time; now the figures proved it. The song also cemented Snow Patrol's status as one of the leading exponents of lighters-aloft, eyes-closed,[59] emotional rock – or at least, it appeared to.

[59] Or not, as their best-selling album has it.

In truth, 'Chasing Cars' was an outlier – an accessible way into Snow Patrol's invigorating and often decidedly strange back catalogue. In an interview with *The Guardian* to follow up the story, lead singer Gary Lightbody described it as 'emotionally open ... it's also unabashedly a love song, and we don't really have any others'. For those who only knew Snow Patrol through 'Chasing Cars' and its artistic twin, 2003's 'Run', that may have seemed an odd statement. Surely the band who had captured the nation's stereos so comprehensively must have more in their emotional arsenal? Yet those more familiar with the band's output knew better. Much like Travis before them, it had taken a while for Snow Patrol to establish a signature sound – their breakthrough album, *Final Straw*, was their third. 2001, the year we pick up their story, found the band at a transitional rather than definitive stage. Though they're not particularly considered part of the acoustic movement, the album Snow Patrol released that year, *When It's All Over We Still Have To Clear Up*, is worth examining for where it would take them next. It may not contain anything approaching their biggest hits, but it is still interesting to consider, especially in the context of the airwave-conquering achievements that lay ahead.

Founding members Lightbody and Mark McClelland, both originally from Northern Ireland, met on their first day at the University of Dundee in 1994, and began writing music together – Lightbody would later note that 'we went to Scotland to form a Northern Irish band'. The pair, along with original drummer Michael Morrison, clicked instantly. Within weeks they had named themselves Shrug, and played shows in various Dundee venues, going on to release a 6-track EP, *The Yogurt vs. Yogurt Debate*, in early 1995. Having quickly built a loyal following in the city, the EP sold well, attracting the attentions of Jeepster Records, who had recently added Belle and Sebastian to their books. Jeepster helped Shrug to record two more demo tapes, signing a management contract with the band in the process. Following a legal challenge from an American band of the same name, Shrug started 1997 as Polarbear. They also shuffled their lineup after Morrison sadly suffered a breakdown; Richard Colburn from Belle and Sebastian deputised while the band cast around for a new sticksman. Jonny Quinn, previously of the Belfast-based Disraeli Gears, and a friend of the band, was persuaded to relocate to Dundee, joining the lineup in time for their next release. Electric Honey, riding high on the success of Belle and Sebastian's classic *Tigermilk* the previous year, took the band on, putting out a well-received Polarbear EP entitled *Starfighter Pilot*. The title track survived the band's second name change, to Snow Patrol, after another dispute over name usage from Jane's Addiction bassist Eric Avery. As Quinn recalls in an interview with *Faze*, 'For the longest time, one of our best friends couldn't remember our band name, so he came around and called us Snow Patrol... So we decided to replace Polarbear with Snow Patrol, but our buddy has just gotten used to calling us Polarbear and we had to break it to him that he should go back to calling us Snow Patrol instead.'

Snow Patrol then relocated from Dundee to the more cosmopolitan surrounds of Glasgow. They set about writing and recording their first record, and continued to play shows in a thriving scene that was home to countless notable bands at the time including Belle and Sebastian, Mogwai and Arab Strap – many of whom were destined to collaborate with Lightbody in later years. Nevertheless, Snow Patrol's debut collection, 1998's *Songs for Polarbears* – released on Jeepster after the band expanded their deal with the company – couldn't be much further from the incarnation of the band that most people know today.

As with so many guitar bands of the mid-nineties, Sebadoh and Pavement provided the primary influences on *Polarbears*. There are echoes of Malkmus & co.'s erratic slacker rock everywhere, as well as beat-led experiments and more abstract jams that, while occasionally intense, don't leave much of an impression beyond that of a band enthusiastically finding their feet. The lineup still included an in-house DJ at gigs. Yet even on this lopsided set, there were signs of what was to come: 'Mahogany', with its spacious lead guitar line and Lightbody's affecting Lou Barlow-esque vocals, suggested a nascent sensitive side to the young upstarts. In a 2008 interview with *Rolling Stone*, Lightbody highlights Barlow's writing as a key influence, describing him as 'really, really good at writing about the cracks in between relationships ... There's a lot of beauty in what he does, and a lot of harmony as well.' There would be time enough for tenderness, though – it was the single 'Velocity Girl' which provided the clearest indication of where Snow Patrol were headed next. Nonchalant, slyly hypnotic and notably quieter than much of the rest of the album, it pared back the slacker stylings, arriving instead in the territory occupied by more studied American acts like Death Cab for Cutie or American Analog Set. 'Velocity Girl' raised the intriguing possibility of what those bands might sound like when fed through the sardonic, self-deprecating filter of late-nineties Scotland.

The reaction to *Songs For Polarbears* from the press was one of fondness rather than awe. *Drowned in Sound*'s assertion that the band were 'never going to be big, and rightly so' was a good example of the prevailing mood. At this stage at least, Snow Patrol were simply a neat addition to a group of spirited, literate indie outfits, including the likes of The Delgados, Spearmint and Ballboy. As with so many of the now-huge performers in this book, mainstream success seemed, for the moment, like a distant prospect.

Snow Patrol's second album for Jeepster, *When It's All Over We Still Have To Clear Up*, was an altogether more coherent effort than *Songs for Polarbears*. It consolidated the sound the band had gestured towards with 'Velocity Girl', often to dazzling effect, and provided a glimpse of the band's future fortunes. Perhaps the most striking change from *Polarbears* comes from Lightbody's vocals, which are clearer and boast greater range. 'One Night is Not Enough' exemplified this: where early Snow Patrol might have overcomplicated matters, this version wrings maximum emotion from the chorus with devastating efficiency; comparisons to Sebadoh were again not unfounded. *When It's All Over* found Lightbody more focused lyrically, too, with *Pitchfork*'s retrospective review of the 2005 reissue noting that, 'Where his band's debut, *Songs for Polar Bears* [sic], tested out a broad expanse of subject material, *When It's All Over* finds Lightbody discovering his strength as an observer of relationships.' In other words, Snow Patrol were beginning a shift from specificity to universality, mirroring the artistic journey of the band who became their closest contemporaries: Coldplay. Later albums would continue that trend, to spectacular effect.

When It's All Over's best moment, 'An Olive Grove Facing the Sea', happens deep into its runtime, as if Snow Patrol have been assessing the best angle from which to approach it. Lightbody appears to agree, describing it as the 'stand-out track' in an interview with *Frame* to promote the album in 2000. The song could easily be viewed as a rehearsal for 'Chasing Cars',[60] and features Lightbody's voice at its best: clambering above the muted brass and languid guitars that propel the verse, then leaning into a pristine chorus. It feels like a revelatory moment; a first attempt at the kind of ballad favoured by many of the artists Snow Patrol were by now beginning to emulate.

The *Pitchfork* review in part echoes my own feelings about *When It's All Over*, calling it 'in retrospect ... a trial run for *Final Straw*'. But there is more to it than that – it deserves to be seen on its own terms, as a bold step forward, a statement of both ambition and readiness. Nevertheless, it seemed Snow Patrol still had work to do to convince the press, who bemoaned their 'overwhelming politeness' and called for a bolder approach. Jeepster dropped the band from its list. To his credit, Lightbody chose to take positives from the setback, evidently inspiring him to further creative heights. He reportedly sold his record collection to pay the rent and keep Snow Patrol afloat; the band had cost Jeepster an estimated £250,000. 'We spent 10 years making records that 6000 people bought,' says Lightbody. A rethink was required, and change was already in the works for the band by the turn of the millennium – but not before a little detour.

Fittingly, a Lou Barlow gig in Glasgow was the setting for a chance meeting of several members of key bands from the scene, including Arab Strap, Mogwai and Belle and Sebastian. Lightbody, apparently frustrated by Snow Patrol's lack of progress, floated the idea of forming a supergroup to record an album together; the resulting project, The Reindeer Section, was an enticing prospect. As well as those in attendance at the Barlow gig, the group eventually boasted a sprawling line-up including members of Alfie, Idlewild, Belle and Sebastian, Teenage Fanclub, Mull Historical Society and The Vaselines. The first Reindeer Section album, *Y'all Get Scared Now, Ya Hear?* (2001) was a triumph. A follow-up, with an even longer list of collaborators, *Son of Evil Reindeer* (2002), followed just ten months later. As it transpired, The Reindeer Section proved a convenient outlet for the more doggedly quirky side of Lightbody's output.

[60] Or a dry 'Run', if you will.

When Snow Patrol reconvened, and having added singer-songwriter Iain Archer to their ranks,[61] they were eyeing a prize much bigger than the confirmation of their peers.

All the while, it seems, Gary Lightbody had been repositioning Snow Patrol in his mind, and two key developments now helped them move up a rung. Firstly, they secured a major label deal with Black Lion, a small subsidiary of Polydor. It was a move that allowed them to recruit a modish, up-and-coming pop producer in Garret 'Jacknife' Lee (who became the band's regular collaborator, and would go on to work with R.E.M., U2 and The Killers). Lee reportedly encouraged Snow Patrol in a more commercial direction, a move made easier by the set of songs Lightbody brought to the *Final Straw* sessions: concise, bouncy pop songs like 'Spitting Games' and 'Wow' were propulsive rushes that recalled no band so much as their Northern Irish counterparts, Ash.[62] But it was the band's first big ballad, 'Run', that stood out in the sessions – a sleeping giant of a song that was about to be awoken.

'Spitting Games' was the first single released, intended to reintroduce the band to listeners ahead of the album. And although it failed to crack the Top 50 (skimming it at 54), it was hailed as something of an indie classic – enough ears were now pricking up to hasten Snow Patrol's ascent towards the major leagues. *Final Straw* itself followed in August 2003, with critics admiring Snow Patrol's new-found confidence. *Shaking Through*'s review hailed 'the most direct and aggressive album yet', and tellingly noticed 'a clear and decisive bid for the kind of wide mainstream appeal enjoyed by the Coldplays of the world'. Yet by Christmas, sales of *Final Straw* were still disappointingly sluggish, with Snow Patrol seemingly unable to raise their public profile. The release of 'Run', and a reissue of *Final Straw* under the Fiction imprint, in February 2004, would change all

[61] An acclaimed singer and songwriter in his own right, Archer knew Jonny Quinn from their time together in Disraeli Gears. He would go on to experience critical successes with solo albums *Flood the Tanks* (2004) and *Magnetic North* (2006), eventually starring alongside Lightbody in the supergroup Tired Pony, which also featured R.E.M.'s Peter Buck and Scott McCaughey.
[62] Ash themselves underwent a phenomenal resurgence during this period, with 2001's *Free All Angels* appearing alongside The Reindeer Section at the business end of many end-of-year rankings. The band's lead singer and songwriter Tim Wheeler also won the Ivor Novello Award for Best Contemporary Pop Song that year, for 'Shining Light'.

that. 'Run' was an unmitigated smash, propelling Snow Patrol at last into the public consciousness, much in the way 'Why Does It Always Rain On Me' and 'Yellow' had in 1999 and 2000. The chart data for the song is testament to its continued popularity: having reached the Top Five upon its initial release, it actually re-entered the Top 30 as recently as 2008, spending several weeks back in the Top 100, and continues to dip in and out to this day. Finally, Snow Patrol had climbed above their indie counterparts to join Travis and Coldplay in the upper echelons of mainstream popularity. Lightbody recalls the sudden acceleration of the band's fortunes in an interview with Ulster University's Life Stories series in 2019. 'In December 2003 we played a gig in High Wycombe in a bar that is a strip club during the day, they unscrew the stripper pole and you set up on the stage, we played to 15 people, seven of which were in the support band, that is how good things were going. The following March we did our next gig in London and played the Shepherd's Bush Empire to 3,000 people and everything just changed in a heartbeat.'

As for *When It's All Over We Still Have To Clear Up*, it seems destined to be viewed as a stepping stone to greater things. Yet it's important to remember that without it, Snow Patrol wouldn't be where they are today. It gave them space to experiment, to push their sound forward; to risk the anthemic. Snow Patrol's sequence of early albums is a satisfying musical evolution because it feels natural, each work gaining them new admirers and sonically paving the way for the next – and in Gary Lightbody, they boast an ambitious frontman just as willing to innovate and sacrifice as Chris Martin is with Coldplay. 'Chasing Cars' may have become a radio staple, but Snow Patrol's is a body of work that rewards those willing to peer beneath their shiny surfaces.

4. 'NAM' and the Manifesto Down the Back of the Sofa

Kings of Convenience – *Quiet is the New Loud*
Turin Brakes – *The Optimist LP*
Kathryn Williams – *Little Black Numbers*

The rapid technological advances that characterised the turn of the century were always going to prompt mixed reactions. The emergence of easy to use file-sharing programs like Napster, which operated between 1999 and 2001 before hitting the buffers over copyright infringement, and relaunching legally again in 2004, allowed both musicians and fans to branch out as never before. Now, they could create and consume in an environment less defined by their immediate surroundings, and a colossal range of music was readily downloadable, no longer bound by clunky physical formats. At the same time, the comparatively sluggish dial-up internet connection introduced in the nineties was gradually being replaced by a much faster proposition: broadband. First installed in March 2000 on Goldsmith Road in Gillingham, broadband was then rolled out around the UK. By 2006, it was estimated that 13 million users had made the switch. And while this was hardly the robotic future predicted by the disconcertingly well-spoken child stars of a 1966 edition of *Tomorrow's World* ('computers are taking over now, computers and automation ... in the year 2000 there just won't be enough jobs to go around'),[63] the newly-christened 'noughties' already felt significantly more than ten years ahead of 1990. Yet in the eyes of some artists, such advanced connectivity was also fostering *disconnection*. Did a faster, louder, less analogue planet necessarily indicate progress? One emergent duo from Bergen, Norway, led a valiant charge away from the digital maelstrom. What could be more convenient, they argued, than two people with guitars?

Kings of Convenience's 2001 debut album, *Quiet is the New Loud* — the title that, as you may have gathered by now, inspired this book — was not just an uncannily pretty acoustic debut. It was wedded to a set of principles that its creators still stand by today.[64]

[63] One particularly perspicacious child hits the nail on the head, though: 'People will be regarded as statistics more than as actual people.'
[64] Remember, they hail from the country that introduced the world to 'slow TV'.

The pair's patience, perseverance and calm spoke of a life lived at a pace dictated *by* them, rather than *for* them. In turn, their fans have also required patience: the Kings have only ever released three studio albums under the name, although both members have been involved in multiple side projects.

Their closest UK equivalent at the time arrived at a similar stripped-back attitude via a different route, and not to such an extreme as their Scandinavian counterparts: after experimenting with soundtrack music, Turin Brakes gravitated towards songs that harked back to the sun-bleached early knockings of the Laurel Canyon set, wrapped up in self-deprecating, unmistakably modern lyrics. The trailblazing career of Kathryn Williams began at this point, too, as her debut album *Dog Leap Stairs* (1999) drew breathless comparisons to folk royalty – despite her insistence that she 'fall[s] down the back of the sofa' with regard to genre. (The same could be said of many of the artists in this book – arguably the one thing uniting them is their refusal to be categorised.) Dozens of others – including Tom McRae, Starsailor, Grand Drive and Gemma Hayes in the UK; Damien Rice in Ireland; and latterly Brendan Benson and Ray LaMontagne in the US – were also swept, willingly or not, into the folds of a new genre: the 'New Acoustic Movement'. The years immediately following the millennium would represent its zenith.

In addition to these newer artists, several acoustic or otherwise quiet 'heritage acts' experienced a revival in both influence and sales during the period, adding validity and momentum to this tenuous movement. In particular, the tragically curtailed careers of Eva Cassidy and Nick Drake both underwent renewed critical and public attention, thanks to reissues of their immaculate work. That pre-millennium atmosphere of rampant nostalgia was morphing into something else: the noughties would prove to be a time in which our addiction to the past met consumer culture head-on, with reissues, reunions and remakes becoming the norm. In *Retromania,* his excellent account of the phenomenon, Simon Reynolds describes the decade: 'If the pulse of NOW felt weaker with each passing year, that's because in the 2000s the pop present became ever more crowded out by the past.'

Further bolstering this craze for rediscovery were the *Acoustic* compilations, released on CD by V2/Echo over five volumes between 2002 and 2005. They briefly acted as an indie equivalent to *Now That's What I Call Music!*, and their tracklists reflected the curiously jumbled nature of the scene: emergent prospects like Ben Christophers and Martha Wainwright were cheerfully thrown in with their jangly predecessors (Tim Buckley, Big Star), as well as representatives from the chillout stable (Morcheeba, Zero 7). The cognitive dissonance of hearing 'Brown Eyed Girl' followed by an acoustic version of My Vitriol's 'Always: Your Way' was severe. Despite their hodgepodge construction, however, the collections were hugely successful, attracting both the younger 'New Acoustic' fans, and those old enough to remember it the first time around. But was this new-found desire for 'authentic' and 'organic' musicianship merely nostalgia for an older, simpler time – or was it a more complex reaction to a world that only seemed to be speeding up?

★★★

KINGS
OF
CONVENIENCE
QUIET IS
THE NEW
LOUD

Kings of Convenience's association with the nascent New Acoustic Movement was coincidental – despite their debut album's title summing up the period better than any other phrase. In truth, the Norwegian duo happened to be making a similar kind of music in a different part of Europe at just the right time, but they found themselves comfortably at home in post-millennium Britain, alongside the likes of Alfie, Coldplay, Turin Brakes and Badly Drawn Boy. Yet they have always remained outliers, careful to distance themselves from the industry. With their ultra-mannered harmonics and close vocal layering, reminiscent of Simon and Garfunkel,[65] theirs has always felt like a more elevated path. As such, *Quiet is the New Loud* has gained a reputation as a kind of totem for the New Acoustic Movement; a high watermark of calm.

[65] Despite the inevitable comparisons, The Kings' Eirik Bøe insists the pair never really listened to Simon & Garfunkel until after the release of *Quiet is the New Loud*.

116

Eirik Glambek Bøe and Erlend Øye met in 1990 at the age of 15 at school in Bergen. Eirik describes the episode, which hints at the precision that would later define their work:

> Our first encounter happened in the natural science lesson... the teacher asked the class what the highest mountain is. I raised my hand and said, 'Everest: 8848 metres.' Then I heard a boy in the back of the classroom correcting me: 'That answer is wrong. Recent satellite measurements have shown that Everest is in fact 8858 metres.' I turned around and saw Erlend for the first time. Later it turned out the new measurements were wrong. Everest is still 8848 metres.[66]

The pair came from slightly different backgrounds: Eirik remembers a house full of music, whereas '[Erlend] had never been part of an environment where music was the most important thing, but he seemed very keen to be'. Erlend would go on to form Skog ('Forest'), a psychedelic folk outfit, in 1992. Eirik joined their ranks a year later, and the band released an EP, *Tom Tids Tale*, in 1996; it would prove to be the band's only recorded effort. By 1997, Erlend and Eirik were operating as a duo, and in 1998 Erlend dropped out of Peachfuzz, the band he had joined after Skog, to focus on the newly-christened Kings of Convenience, a reference to the ease with which they could move their new, simplified setup around. The band played their first 'proper' UK show in May 1998, at the Poetry Café in Covent Garden, the first of five shows they would play in the country that year. 'We were booked to play there by a friend of a friend. And about ten of their friends turned up. I don't think anyone was particularly impressed, but we were already pretty confident ourselves. The songs we played were mostly songs that would be on *Quiet is the New Loud*.' Debs Wild, who encountered the band at the time too, also recalls being taken by their sound, and as we've seen, her instincts were usually spot on. 'They were making music that was true to themselves, and where they were from, and their scene. They were carving out their own little thing. You can sometimes tell when artists are being clichéd, trying to "create"

---

[66] Author email interview with Eirik Glambek Bøe, November 2019. All subsequent quotes taken from this interview unless otherwise stated.

something, and I always preferred bands like Kings of Convenience where it's an organic thing.'

One of the shows that Erlend's band Peachfuzz had played in their short lifespan was at In The City in Manchester, as the first Norwegian band ever to appear on the festival's bill. Erlend would return with Eirik just a year later, promoting a demo of songs recorded under the KoC banner. The duo played In The City's closing party in 1998; it seems to be where their love affair with Manchester and its musicians started to blossom. While in Manchester they stayed with Alfie cellist Matt McGeever, and in doing so became friendly with the rest of the band (particularly Lee Gorton), along with Damon Gough and Andy Votel of Twisted Nerve, and members of Doves and I Am Kloot.[67] It was the start of a fruitful and symbiotic relationship which saw the Kings drawn into the community described in chapter two: playing at each others' gigs and on record, and covering each others' hits.[68] Having found the industry receptive to their demo, the duo signed with Source,[69] who would acquire Turin Brakes two years later, but there was a slightly unusual stipulation in the Kings' contract. They made sure that they could put out three singles preceding the album ('Toxic Girl', 'Failure' and 'Brave New World') on their original Norwegian label, Éllet Records, all of which came out in 1999; and an eponymous album, made up of recordings already undertaken in Bergen, on Kindercore Records in the USA.[70] Quoted in Ørjan Nilsson's excellent history of the album, Eirik explains the move, saying 'the idea was to start at smaller companies in order to build a foundation of dedicated music fans'. The first release on Source was the five-song EP *Playing Live in a Room*, which contained bare-bones versions of 'Toxic Girl' and 'Singing Softly to Me'. The time came to record an album, and Source set the band up with – you've guessed it – Ken Nelson. Keen to revisit some of the tracks from

---

[67] All of whom are thanked in the sleevenotes of *Quiet is the New Loud*, along with 'all the good people in Manchester'.

[68] They covered Badly Drawn Boy's 'Once Around the Block' as the B-side to 'Toxic Girl'; Alfie covered their 'Failure' on the remix album *Versus*.

[69] Originally founded in France, Source was already home to electro-pop duo Air, and would open a permanent UK office in 1999. The label's founder Philippe Ascoli once described Kings of Convenience in a BBC interview as 'Belle and Sebastian meets Peter Sellers'.

[70] Although this release was, at 37 minutes, album-length, the band still consider *Quiet is the New Loud* their official debut.

their Kindercore release, they headed to Liverpool in early 2000 and began work at his Parr Street Studios. Nelson, who was by now becoming the go-to producer for young acoustic bands, was at this point between recording Coldplay's first two albums:

> We were excited to record with Ken ... he had been working with Badly Drawn Boy, who we had played with as backing band, and whose music we really liked. We thought that working with a proper producer in a professional studio would make it easier to record. But it turned out that all the amazing microphones just made it even clearer how clumsy our playing and singing was. We struggled a lot, but in the end Ken made everything sound as good as it could. I don't see how we could have achieved a better result taking our modest skills into account.

The sessions largely went well, but what was supposed to be a fortnight's worth of recording somehow became three months, with some tracks proving harder to pin down than others. Notoriously detail-oriented, the band were finding it difficult to surpass in their eyes the recordings they had made for the Kindercore release, back in the tiny Verteft Studio in Bergen. To break the deadlock, they flew over that record's producer, Morten Arnetvedt, who brought with him the original recordings; these were finessed by Nelson and two of the tracks, 'Toxic Girl' and 'Failure' made the final cut for the album. And what an album it turned out to be.

But before we listen, let's look; the peaceful precision awaiting on *Quiet is the New Loud* even extends to its unmistakable artwork. The front cover consists of a photo taken in Grimseid, just outside of Bergen: Erlend facing down the camera with something approaching a wistful smile; Eirik, eyes closed, clutching his then-girlfriend (now wife), Ina Grung. Norwegian twilight bathes a shoreside cabin in pastel tones. On the centre spread of the CD booklet, gently rippling water, framed by pine trees. Everything suggests taste, restraint, simplicity. And while that's true to a certain extent, *Quiet is the New Loud* is also a debut of surprising momentum and no little musical invention, revealing Kings of Convenience as far more than the sixties folk parodists some critics thought they were dealing with at the time. It's also no surprise that the duo, particularly Øye, went on to work seriously within dance and electronica; their love of pattern and rhythm is clear on this collection. Having said all that, *Quiet is the New Loud* begins with one of the band's most tranquil moments. 'Winning a Battle, Losing the War' unmistakably sets out the KoC stall: close harmonies, gently rueful lyrics, musicianship that blends warmth and exactitude in a way that few have managed before or since. As Eirik says of the time, 'Of course there were people around who sang and played acoustic guitar, but when they went into the studio to record, they would all add all kinds of tracks. We wanted to keep it as simple as possible.' The lyrics invoke the turning of time, renewal, beginnings. 'The sun sets on the war / The day breaks and everything is new'. Fingerpicked, dappled acoustics radiate beautifully from the song's core – like the gentle waves on that lake – and before you know it, you're hooked. Then comes 'Toxic Girl' which, when re-released as a UK single, represented the band's biggest chart hit to date, reaching number 44 in April that year. The bright trumpets and bossa nova-infused guitars of 'Singing Softly to Me' put one more in mind of a sleepy seaside *boteco* than the fjords. The peak of a strong first half is 'I Don't Know What I Can Save You From', with its sinuous lead guitar line – perhaps the most complete and mature effort on *Quiet is the New Loud*, it presages the ultra-refined atmosphere of the Kings' later records.[71] The second half begins with the deceptively adventurous lounge-jazz of 'The Girl From Back Then', which in turn heralds further experiments such as the trance-like repetition on 'Little Kids'. The writing and arrangement on late highlight 'Summer on the Westhill' is particularly strong: strings that permeate without cloying; guitars that resonate just on the right side of New Age; a minor-key section at the end which leaves the whole tantalisingly unresolved. It all suggested that Kings of Convenience, due to the sheer weight of thought they put into every second of their music, were already operating on a higher technical level than their contemporaries. Despite the assurances of its title, and the modesty of its creators, this was the loudest of statements.

[71] I'm thinking in particular of the astonishing 'Homesick' which opens their second album, *Riot on an Empty Street* (2004).

Unfortunately, the early press reactions to the Kings' first UK releases and shows had been – by today's more enlightened standards – borderline ridiculous. Words like 'speccy', 'limp-wristed' and 'quivering bottom lips' attended their early single reviews, perhaps indicative of a critical era that still secretly yearned for the testosterone-fuelled thrust of Britpop. An *NME* review of 'Toxic Girl' labelled them the 'mimsy Viking warlords of NAM'. Yet by the time *Quiet is the New Loud* arrived, there were signs that reviewers were warming to the pair – that, despite the obvious cultural difficulties presented by Erlend wearing oversized glasses, these reclusive Scandinavians might be onto something. RTÉ's review of *Quiet is the New Loud* contained a telling remark gesturing towards the overall appeal of the NAM: 'If quiet is indeed the new loud or black or whatever then Eirik and Erlend are on to a sure winner. A bittersweet pop album to wrap yourself up in when the world feels like a scary place.' In just over six months, it was to become even scarier.

By the spring and summer of 2001, then, Eirik and Erlend were *in* the New Acoustic Movement, even if they were never *of* it. Their artistic vision was always more singular and distilled, looking beyond the immediate pigeonholing of the UK press. For them, their music was one element of a wider lifestyle choice, and 'quiet is the new loud' a tongue-in-cheek motto to simplify it. For Erlend (at least to begin with), it meant a doggedly ascetic approach to his craft. In an interview with Simon Price in *The Independent* early in 2001 he sets out his way of thinking: 'I don't drink, I don't take drugs, I get all my clothes second hand, I live with my parents and I walk everywhere. It allows me to live cheaply, and devote all my time to thinking about my music.' Yet even straight after *Quiet is the New Loud*'s release, it became clear the pair had different paths in mind. Eirik – who perhaps hadn't considered the full implications of being in a touring indie band – was keen to return to his life in Bergen with Ina as soon as possible, having already been in England for a year. Erlend, on the other hand, was now ready to see more of the world. 2001 should have been a triumphant year for the band – instead it proved chaotic and frustrating, with Eirik diagnosed with an illness he later identified as chronic fatigue syndrome. It led to the cancellation of many key tour dates, including several shows with their fellow reluctant NAM-ites, Turin Brakes. Later that year, in protest at US military action in the wake of 9/11, the band announced they were boycotting American shows for the foreseeable future. 'I'm still proud of the Afghanistan protest,' Eirik says, 'a lot of people thought that the invasion was a good idea, but I was proven right.'

Against this backdrop of micro- and macrocosmic upheaval, a remix album of tracks from *Quiet is the New Loud*, entitled *Versus*, suggested further changes. Released just six months after the Kings' debut, it featured reworkings by electronica luminaries including Four Tet, fellow Norwegians Röyksopp and Ladytron. The former's version of 'I Don't Know What I Can Save You From' is particularly effective,[72] and the 'Monte Carlo 1963 Version' of 'Toxic Girl', resplendent with zippy *nouvelle vague* strings, could, as the title suggests, plausibly have been lifted from some forgotten French arthouse film. Some versions stick closely to their source material, others veer wildly away, with varying degrees of success. Alfie's cover version of 'Failure' is a triumph, a clatter of percussion and squalling guitars. Ladytron's ominous version of 'Little Kids', complete with bells, bleeps and a gigantic organ sound, sits uneasily on what is otherwise a soothing collection. *Versus* confirmed that Øye and Bøe were not afraid to experiment and adapt, neither were they overly precious about their music once it had left their hands. Critics largely admired the move, with many seemingly surprised that such a refined and restrained band had given themselves so willingly. *Drowned in Sound* were especially complimentary, awarding the record an 8/10 in their review: 'An apparently nightmarishly cynical exercise in genre-transgressing becomes a vital reminder of the Kings' songwriting genius, far and beyond what the whole "new-acoustic" label suggests.'

In what would prove to be the first in a pattern of separations and reunions, Erlend then stepped away from Kings of Convenience, releasing a more dance-led solo album, *Unrest*, in 2003. The collection had a genesis that made *Quiet is the New Loud* seem positively monastic in comparison: it was recorded in ten different cities with ten different producers. Øye's nomadic nature, which would see him living all over the world for the next decade, before eventually

---

[72] The two acts also worked together on Röyksopp's 'Remind Me', which appeared on their hugely successful debut *Melody A.M.*, released around the same time as *Versus*.

settling in Sicily, was beginning to kick in. Yet there remained an element of the strict self-regulation that had defined *Quiet is the New Loud*. As he relates in an interview with *MusicOMH* in 2003: 'I set myself a deadline of four days to record each track – if I hadn't done that I'd have re-recorded and changed it and it would have taken longer … It was really a discipline.' The emergence of a solo album naturally raised questions about whether the Kings were still a going concern. Yet the two men at the heart of the project have always been relaxed about their status as a band. In the same interview, Erlend simply says that Eirik 'didn't want to be as busy with music just now, and I did'. This wasn't a cynical building up of mystique – simply the plain facts of two lives and all their apparent contradictions. These two unassuming yet uncommonly driven artists are the purest distillation of the movement they accidentally helped to begin – a movement which has only gained in relevance as the world has continued to get faster and louder. As Erlend recalls:

> I still remember the internet that I surfed around on in 1998. It was extremely boring. But even without the internet that we know today, the world then was already very busy and full of distractions. To be able to pursue a thought without getting distracted is something that's getting harder and harder.

Kings of Convenience was only ever meant as one facet of Erlend and Eirik's respective existences – a means to stave off that distraction. Their decision to compartmentalise is quietly radical: for a band to acknowledge that a career in music doesn't have to be the centre of their lives, especially so early on, feels like a revelation usually only reached by outfits after slogging their guts out on the circuit for decades. They have never unduly troubled the charts – but then, it seems the charts have never unduly troubled them.[73] It's also clear they are loved: although they haven't intentionally attained legendary status, their perfectionist attitude to releasing music means that, when new material does arrive, it is met with high excitement. Their fans, much like the band themselves, are always prepared to wait.

★★★

[73] Though they are bona fide stars in their native Norway, and command high chart placings in Italy.

'We toured with Kings of Convenience,' Olly Knights, lead singer of Turin Brakes tells me. 'We were... very different to them, back then.' He smiles. 'We were a lot more chaotic.'[74]

Turin Brakes and the Kings were more than just tour-mates: they were destined to be held up (somewhat uncomfortably) alongside each other in the early 2000s, as leading lights of the New Acoustic Movement.[75] It's true that the duo share much in common with their Norwegian counterparts: the band's core members are old school friends, and their music foregrounds acoustic guitars, precise musicianship and solid songwriting. They both released their debut albums in the UK on the same day, 5th March 2001, on the same record label. Yet *The Optimist LP* deserves to be viewed as a singular effort, and remains appealingly difficult to pin down. Perhaps this

---

[74] Author interview with Olly Knights and Gale Paridjanian, July 2019. All quotes taken from this interview unless otherwise stated.
[75] Their Discogs profile lists them as 'quiet is the new loud folk rock'.

isn't surprising from a band who counted the kaleidoscopic, future-blues visions of Beck and Gomez among their early inspirations, and whose career has seen them expand and innovate with each new release.

Knights and schoolfriend Gale Paridjanian formed Turin Brakes (a name pulled at random from a dictionary) in south London in 1999. The pair met at Macauley School in Clapham, and spent their childhoods immersed in music, singing in choirs, playing various instruments and recording themselves on four-track recorders – as well as listening endlessly to their idol, Chuck Berry. Knights recalls getting a 'ridiculous flying V' guitar as an early Christmas present; Paridjanian recalls exotic instruments hanging from his living room wall, and working in a guitar shop during his apparently misspent teenage years. Then, as he told an *Independent* interview in 2002: 'I had this sort of emotional crisis where my brain suddenly said: "Start using your hands; stop drinking; stop being a waster."' It just so happened that Knights was studying film at St. Martin's College at the time (the same course taken by Jarvis Cocker some years earlier), and was looking for a soundtrack for a short film he was working on. The pair's musical project was born, and they began committing their efforts more seriously to tape. By chance, these caught the ear of manager Phil Passera, who overheard Gale's now-wife Miriam playing a demo in her car on the way to Brighton. Passera sensed the duo were onto something and decided to fund a release using a £500 enterprise loan.

'Before [meeting Passera] we'd honestly just been having fun, recording little oddball folk songs in between larger scale experimental cinematic things. Phil encouraged us to focus on the folky bits,' says Knights. The result of that focus, *The Door EP*, released on Anvil in August 1999, was well received – and thanks to Passera's electronica and hip-hop connections, the pair found themselves tentatively thrust into the now-thriving chillout genre. The signals were promising from critics: one early gig review ends with 'Go and see them play. Give them the devotion they deserve.' A dozen major labels were soon circling, with the band eventually settling on Source in 2000, a label who were fast becoming key players in the UK acoustic scene, having already snapped up Kings of Convenience. 'We liked [Source founder] Philippe Ascoli … he basically said, "I love you, don't change, I'll bring the mainstream to you." We signed on a Friday, and were making *The Optimist LP* by the next Monday.'

Even then, Turin Brakes were still only beginning to find an identity. 'We went into the studio [to record *The Optimist LP*] thinking we were going to do this lo-fi, surreal thing, and we found a lot of stuff coming out emotionally while we were making it. We hadn't really learned to write songs in any classic sense, but for some reason – maybe under a bit of pressure to come up with something bigger after we got signed – we seemed to be able to create very raw emotive songs that had a touch of the classic about them,' says Olly. 'I think it took us both by surprise.' Gale remembers the duo still having the cinematic element on their minds: 'We talked a lot about it being a film soundtrack … something you couldn't quite place but made sense. A future and a past all in one.' By drawing deeply from both, it seemed the pair had hit upon a winning formula. After the band wrapped up the sessions, Source sat on the recordings, asking the band to build their fanbase further before they could be released. As such, Turin Brakes hit the road with Rob Allum (drums), Eddie Myer (bass) and Phil Marten (keys) for much of 2000. They toured heavily, building a profile around their first two EP releases for Source: *The State of Things* in July, and *Fight or Flight* in October. In another development indicative of how the band was being sold at the time, a version of 'Future Boy' appeared on a 12" EP released that year on Mind Horizon, along with UK hip-hop luminaries DJ Skitz and Rodney P. They also played their first major festivals, Reading and Leeds, at the end of July – just three weeks after Coldplay had hit the top spot with *Parachutes.*

The Optimist LP finally appeared in March 2001 after Source re-released 'The Door' as a pre-album single. Just like *Quiet is the New Loud*, it is an exercise in hushed subversion: Turin Brakes' unassuming airs acted as a smokescreen, allowing them to attempt lyrical invention on a scale that their peers often shied away from. It's a quality of Turin Brakes' writing that Knights attributes to his art school education, as well as his love of great lyricists like Bob Dylan and Elliott Smith: 'I think the experimental ideas of the art school scene really helped keep us just on the right side of ambiguous – it helped me have the confidence to enjoy the surreal meanings that could come from juxtaposed lyrics.' Certainly lines as cryptic as 'Like a man with glasses catching a sunbeam and burning the skin of a kid / Hyperreal fragments disturbing the stagnance of almighty fear' don't often crop up in opening songs on debut albums, but these are wrapped in such tender instrumental clothing it takes several listens to realise you're listening to something quite dark indeed. 'Feeling Oblivion' opens with a single, pure note – suggestive of the idyllic June day described in the lyrics. Yet this is a tale from a loner's perspective, yearning for escape; a recurring theme on the record. Coded observations, paired with accounts of travel and movement, also lend a road-trip feel to many of the songs on *The Optimist*. But these are journeys recorded through a cracked, millennial lens, preoccupied with the futuristic. That mood pervades across the band's first breakout hit 'Underdog (Save Me)' ('put one foot on the road now / where the cyborgs are driving') and on late-album sparkler 'Mind Over Money', which boasts a beautiful high-wire vocal line from Knights, Paridjanian's guitar drawing forth a nagging, Neil Young-esque melody. 'Keep blood on the inside and nowhere else / Up on a shelf, that's where I need to be' is again typical of their lyrical approach: clinical yet warm, straightforward yet strange. Beyond those singles, there are still more outsiders: the unsettling 'Future Boy' is told from the point of view of an alien visitor to Earth who is 'taking babies back with me'; 'Starship' imagines a rocket launch from a dusty desert landscape. Concluding track 'The Optimist' perhaps reveals the source of these imaginings – its protagonist possesses a 'cracked skull with a creepy mind inside' who ultimately realises 'there's no escape, lonely planet'. This is isolated American highway music spiked with the English eerie of John Wyndham or H.G. Wells – and it works, beautifully. Is that blurry glow on the record's cover a passing headlight, or a UFO? Turin Brakes' abstraction means that, pleasingly, we can decide for ourselves.

Critics were equally taken with *The Optimist*, with Dan Kilian's *Pitchfork* review among the warmest: 'Dear me, it's a pretty album, with a melancholy that's – of course – unaffected. It has a softness that soothes without deflating.' 'Unaffected' is the key word here; critics were now hankering after a sound that was *real*, after a wearying decade of British showmanship. Gale sketches the period perfectly: 'There was a lot of macho and a lot of electronic music that was really about youth and going out, much of which we enjoyed – but there was another way of expressing the time, with the acoustic instruments we had at home. It did seem that people were trying to find something beyond the pomp and bravado.' Olly agrees: 'Neither of us were very into Britpop at all really ... it all seemed a bit pompous and too styled. I think we got lucky with timing, because it seems lots of other people felt the same.' A breathless 9/10 *NME* review described the album as 'feverish, contemplative, nostalgic ... dustbowl folk music refracted through inner-city noise'.

By the end of the summer of 2001, it seemed Turin Brakes' coronation with both press and public was complete. It had been a sensational year for the band, and sales of *The Optimist LP* grew over the summer thanks to a string of high-profile festival appearances. The album eventually achieved gold status and spent almost six months in the Top 40 (though it never climbed higher than 27). '72', a re-recorded version of the album's 'Emergency 72', saw them narrowly miss out on their third Top 40 single in a row. *The Optimist LP* was also nominated for that year's Mercury Prize, along with several other artists from the acoustic crop, including Ed Harcourt's impressive *Here Be Monsters* and Tom McRae's fine eponymous debut.[76] The accolade was a considerable achievement: for an album of such homespun beginnings to be placed alongside comparative veterans Radiohead and Super Furry Animals must have been immensely gratifying. The prize went to PJ Harvey's majestic *Stories from the City, Stories from the Sea* but the ceremony, which took place on 11th September 2001, was of course overshadowed by events elsewhere. Things were about to change for the whole world, in

[76] McRae's album was released on the newly-formed DB Records, headed up by experienced A&R man Dave Bates. McRae's story partially mirrors David Gray's: having reached the age of 29 without finding a deal, he thought it was never going to happen and was 'ready to give up'. He tells me, 'The acoustic movement felt like a breath of fresh air because there was no clutter, nothing to sift through ... I thought I'd signed with a brand new indie label, but by the time I'd finished making the album I was licensed to Sony/BMG. That was a bit of a headfuck!' McRae's obvious talent combined with Bates's marketing nous meant that the album achieved huge critical success, earning McRae a Brit Award nomination alongside his Mercury nod. The *Evening Standard* described him as 'an angel singing the devil's tunes'. As well as steering McRae through the early years of his career, Bates also took a chance on an exciting young band from Brighton called The Electric Soft Parade.

tragic circumstances.[77] As Knights recalls: 'The day it happened we were in camera rehearsals [for the televised prize ceremony]. We'd just finished our play-through, and the camera guys all just stopped talking. One of them beckoned us over and got us to look into his camera eyepiece, where he was being fed the image of the first tower on fire.'

Apart from the pronounced horrors of its immediate aftermath, one of the longer-term effects of 9/11 was the precautionary grounding of both inbound and outbound US flights for weeks after the event. Turin Brakes were among those affected: their planned tour of the States, supporting the Stereophonics and beginning in New York, was cancelled. They had been due to fly out on 13th September. Knights, like so many other artists at the time, felt a shift in the air: 'It signalled the end of the party in some ways; put everything back into perspective.' And though they opened for the ever-popular James in support of the Brian Eno-produced *Pleased to Meet You* (2001) on their UK tour in December, the year ended – as it did for the world – on a subdued note.

The band reconvened in early 2002 to work on the follow-up to *The Optimist LP*, then travelled to Los Angeles to record with Beck and Air producer Tony Hoffer that summer. The result was 2003's *Ether Song*, a collection that saw the Turin Brakes sound expand dramatically.

> At the time I remember us having the conversation, that if we tried to do *The Optimist* part two, we'd be stuck doing that forever. You have to remember what a huge influence bands like Radiohead, and even Pink Floyd, still had on other British bands – even if you hated them, they made sure each record had a new identity … it kept other bands on their toes to be musically progressing at all costs.

Gale also recalls an ambition to move forward with their sound. 'There was the NAM, that we didn't feel totally comfortable being in. We felt more Beck, an acoustic Nirvana or Sebadoh, than folk … there was an acoustic punk in us.' If *The Optimist LP* had been about

[77] As it happened, Harvey was touring the US at the time, and was staying in Washington when The Pentagon was attacked.

a yearning for adventure among the stars, *Ether Song* – as suggested by the title – saw Turin Brakes achieve lift-off and embrace the upper atmosphere. There's even a band logo incorporating a rocket ship on the cover. Coming almost exactly two years after *The Optimist LP*, their return proved a welcome one. Lead single 'Painkiller' hit the dizzy heights of number five in the charts, and *Ether Song* would provide the band with the first of their two Top Ten LPs to date, reaching number four. The closing suite of the album, incorporating downbeat final number 'Rain City' and leading to the astonishingly supple Jeff Buckley-esque title track, is perhaps its most remarkable asset. *Ether Song* set them on a path that they still walk today, with the restless stirrings of their debut album still drawing people in: 'People still seem to really resonate with that record … something about it packs a punch.'

Although neither Kings of Convenience nor Turin Brakes felt particularly attached to the NAM, the movement had found its twin peaks in *Quiet is the New Loud* and *The Optimist LP*. Yet unlike the Kings, whose relationship has always been complicated by what they call periods of 'disagreement', Olly and Gale remain close. Reflecting on their career for *Songwriting* magazine in 2015, Knights attributes that friendship as key to their success – both of which continue to this day:

> I don't know if it's because we tried really hard or we were just really lucky, but for some reason the relationship between us has been incredibly strong. It doesn't mean to say that we never get upset with each other, of course we do, but we have this ability to spend incredible amounts of time with each other … I know it sounds corny, but that's literally the reason we're still together as a band. We all feel that we've made some great music, and our best is probably what we've just done.

★★★

Kathryn Williams — LITTLE BLACK NUMBERS

The Union Chapel in Islington is an enormous venue – positively gulp-inducing for first-time artists expecting a village church. On an early autumn afternoon in 2019, sunshine fills its vast space, casting amber light over the red-brick walls. I'm here for a busy daytime gig: children run freely up and down the aisles, and there is a constant flow of people coming and going with cups of coffee and bits of cake, nattering amiably between sets. Towards the end, a trio of songwriters take to the stage, taking it in turns to sing one song each. Some of them are new to this game; it's likely the Union Chapel is their biggest gig so far. Yet all three songs bear the mark of quality and craft – they all could have been sung by older, more experienced heads. Then again, perhaps their maturity is not surprising, because they've been guided by one of the masters of the craft: Kathryn Williams. These three songwriters are graduates of workshops she now oversees with Squeeze songwriter Chris Difford.

Williams has invited an array of well-known friends along today – including Colin MacIntyre of Mull Historical Society, Romeo and Michele Stodart of The Magic Numbers, and Difford himself. At the end of the show, everyone joins Williams for a cover of a Neil Young song. As she stands centre stage accepting applause from her audience and peers, it's remarkable to see a further flourishing of an artist who, at one time, would ask people to leave the room before she could even play a note.

Now a veteran songwriter of some standing, Williams recently released her *Anthology* box set, which takes in her ten studio albums over two decades. Yet for all her obvious artistic achievement you feel she won't be satisfied until she and her female counterparts achieve equal footing in the music industry. Her second album, *Little Black Numbers*, was a groundbreaking work in that regard: self-released, and recorded on a tiny budget, it earned a Mercury Prize nomination and a major label deal for Williams, as well as providing an example for self-starting women in a business – and a culture – still overwhelmingly dominated by men. It helps, too, that *Little Black Numbers* is a joy: as subtle, wry and melodic as anything she has ever recorded.

Born in Liverpool in 1974, Williams comes from a musical family: her father was the singer in a folk band, stepping down when Kathryn and her sister came along.[78] She recalls a house full of sound: 'I listened to a lot of Paul Simon and Dylan, mum was into Dr Hook and Janis Joplin, and my dad was into the more folky stuff. So we had a lot going on there … I think probably the biggest thing for me was that music became a solace quite quickly.'[79] Williams was bullied at a 'rough school', and remembers using music as a shield throughout her early years: 'I used to put my mum and dad's big brown headphones on and listen to Janis Joplin before I went to school – that gave me the courage to face school every day … I realised the magic of music.'

That realisation began to flourish while living in a shared house after her studies wound down. Her housemates, upon hearing her efforts on guitar through the walls (despite 'not being taught chords

[78] He was replaced, interestingly, by the playwright Willy Russell.
[79] Author interview with Kathryn Williams, October 2019. All subsequent quotes taken from this interview unless otherwise stated.

or anything'), booked her on to a songwriters' evening. They had perhaps not fully understood the extent of Williams's apparent reluctance to perform: 'I used to have panic attacks and agoraphobia. I was very, very shy, couldn't sing in front of people.' She remembers not being able to sleep in the lead-up to the evening, 'but I did it. And then the second time, someone from the *NME* came and wrote about me. Then the third time there were people there scouting from record labels.' Suddenly, Williams was hot property, yet she was healthily suspicious of label interest, deciding instead to go her own way. She set up her own imprint instead, Caw Records, and went about recording her first album, recalling her thought process in typically modest fashion: 'People liked my songs and so I thought, "well they must be good…"' They certainly were. Recorded on a miniscule budget (some estimates put it at just £80), *Dog Leap Stairs* (1999) was mainly put together via a combination of donated studio free time and an old four-track owned by Williams:

> When it came to mastering the album, the songs that I'd done on the four-track, the masterer thought it was incredible because the hiss was louder than the music! But it was amazing, because he turned a few knobs and stuff and then suddenly there was this really crisp song without hiss – and it just sounded so real and proper. It was a real discovery – like blowing the dust off something.

Dog Leap Stairs was extremely well reviewed, with *Uncut* paying it the ultimate compliment: 'In 30 years' time they'll be cooing over *Dog Leap Stairs* with the reverence currently afforded to Nick Drake's albums.' The attention enabled Williams to bolster her rudimentary setup: 'An agent called up and said they wanted to be my agent, and [a] press officer, so I quickly got a really good team around us for the label.'

Williams's agent was to prove invaluable, providing another key moment in her career around this time. She was invited at the last minute to play at a Nick Drake tribute night at The Barbican Centre in London. 'I had to choose [which Nick Drake song to play], and someone hadn't chosen "Saturday Sun" or "From the Morning". I love both those songs. So I got there, and there was an orchestra and a big band – I'd been playing for like 50 people before that, and then I was at The Barbican.' It was another leap that Williams didn't feel entirely ready for. 'I remember being backstage and there was David Gray and Bernard Butler, just so many people I knew who were "in music". I just thought "God, I'm out of my depth completely."' It was only thanks to The Barbican's labyrinthine layout that she didn't run away entirely. Convincing herself she still had time to slip away, she put her coat on, grabbed her guitar, and was attempting to find the exit 'when someone grabbed me and said "you're on"'. Despite a minor hiccup ('the first violinist was almost leaned over double, looking at me and nodding to give the signal to start the song'), her appearance was a triumph. 'It's always the way with me on stage – all the other stuff is like being a penguin on land, but as soon as the music starts I'm underwater, totally inside the song. It went by in a flash – and then everyone was standing up and cheering. I couldn't quite believe it.' She was contacted by London Records to record some demos, and resumed work with the producer Head (best known for his work with PJ Harvey at the time) – who had also produced a number of the songs on *Dog Leap Stairs*. The sessions were clearly successful: 'That quickly became the second album.' It was a collection which would change her life.

Little Black Numbers works a similar magic to *Quiet is the New Loud* and *The Optimist LP* almost straight away. The album was recorded reel-to-reel, and as such a soothing warmth hangs over proceedings; the sonic equivalent of a sheepskin coat. 'We Dug A Hole' creaks and weaves; 'Soul to Feet' shuffles along on jazzy shoes; 'Jasmine Hoop' floats on a gently undulating church organ. 'Fell Down Fast' weds a sweetly swaying double bass to Williams's careful sigh, and strings kick in on 'Morning Song' like a sunrise. Closer 'We Came Down from the Trees' boasts a sweetly unsettled melody in the chorus, driving the song onward even as it speaks of deep tiredness. Throughout, Williams's arrangements are braver, more mature and more ambitious than on *Dog Leap Stairs*; it is the sound of an artist finding her groove and revelling in it. Confidence, having previously been such a challenge, now rises from these wise and welcoming songs. It was an album that cried out for recognition – and got it.

Williams scraped together the entry fee for the Mercury Music Prize and entered *Little Black Numbers* into the 2000 contest. Label representatives of that year's entrants were called to a ceremony and Williams, being the label *as well as* the artist, made her way there. 'When [the nomination] was announced, and everyone turned to me ... I ran away and hid in a pub. Not what everyone I was working with wanted me to do! But it just felt a bit too much. Then I was followed around by the BBC for a documentary, I had loads of interviews, I suppose because it was an interesting angle.' By nominating Williams, it felt like the Mercury panel were doing more than giving their customary nod to a relatively unknown folk or jazz act – they were helping to launch an entire career. 'It was massive for me – I think it did more for me than for anyone else that year. I got a major record deal from it, sold 40,000 records out of my bedroom. At the time, I was really very poor – in the lead-up to it, I really wanted that cheque because I needed the money!' It wasn't to be for Williams – but as she acknowledges, with the resulting attention and raised profile it afforded her, 'everyone thinks I won it anyway – and it was an amazing time'. Twenty years later, on her *Anthology* tour, she has been telling a story from the night of the prizegiving, in which she gave career tips to a young Chris Martin:

> I was drunk at the ceremony and I was chatting to Chris, and I said, 'How much did your record [*Parachutes*] cost?' Half a million, or something. I said to him, 'Chris I've got a little bit of advice for you: you're never going to get anywhere or make money spending that much on an album...' Then I saw him a few years later at the BBC – I could see him walking towards me, they were doing *X&Y* then – it had massively blown up for them. I was just cringing, and he said 'Hey Kath! Thanks for the advice.' In a really playful, nice way, but I was like 'Oh, God'.

Williams, unlike many artists at the time, was sanguine about being categorised in the New Acoustic Movement – speaking warmly of Turin Brakes, Tom McRae and Kings of Convenience, and seemingly grateful to be associated with something fresh and new: 'Before that, and since then, I've been labelled as a folk artist. Well – by anyone who isn't in the folk world, I'm called a folk artist, and then shunned by the folk world! ... I fall down the back of the sofa in that respect. I think that's what united a lot of the artists around at that time.' By the time the NAM was in full flow, Williams was also playing regularly in America, and witnessed the emerging New Rock Revolution too, 'hanging out with The Strokes and The Moldy Peaches'. It's easy to see how Williams's work chimed with the anti-folk movement of which Moldy Peaches Adam Green and Kimya Dawson formed the vanguard. Both wanted to move on from their respective songwriting traditions, while keeping the lo-fi, homemade spirit in which the music was made alive. 'We weren't interested in traditional folk – that wasn't what it was, I think we'd all listened to a lot of our parents' records – Neil Young, Joni Mitchell, Bob Dylan, Leonard Cohen – taken inspiration from that and then pushed it forward into the way we wanted to make our music.'

We speak a little about her craft. She studied art at college before settling on music, and the visual has always worked in parallel to her songwriting: 'When I was doing my art degree I would secretly make music and poetry – then when that finished, I kind of fell into the music world, and did art as a secretive thing. So there's always been that availability to do something that's not for public consumption – when it's music, I could do art for my own pleasure, and vice versa. And I quite like that, having that outlet, because if I didn't have art then I'd have way too many songs.' She has always been wary of the trope that women always write songs from life; are somehow incapable of fictive imagination – whereas men are permitted unlimited flights of fancy:

> When you're a female artist and you write songs, people would naturally assume that you were taking excerpts from your diary and putting them on ... but as a writer, you imagine things and explore things, just as you would with painting. I don't think people think Elton John actually *is* a Rocket Man... but then people think 'White Flag' by Dido must have come exactly from a relationship breaking down. Even something like *Blood on the Tracks*, which is a break-up album – that's the momentum, but as with all things, if you're writing a novel or a poem or a song, you have an idea of what you want to do, but then the artistic structure and pathway is changed by the actual writing of it.

Those thoughts are at the forefront of Williams's mind these days, as she both takes stock of her own work, and helps to create new art with others. You can hear her gentle impact in the music of her protégées at the Union Chapel. It's a fitting legacy for one of our most underrated songwriters, and *Little Black Numbers* is just one of countless treasures in her still-growing catalogue.

5. A Curtain or a Star
The Interior Visions of Lowgold,
Mull Historical Society and The Electric Soft Parade

Lowgold – *Just Backward of Square*
Mull Historical Society – *Loss*
The Electric Soft Parade – *Holes in the Wall*

On *The Hour of Bewilderbeast*, Badly Drawn Boy had proved that a microscopic study of one's inner world could result in modern and successful music-making. Others were set to follow, and over the next few years, further introspective and off-kilter visions emerged from their creators' heads and into the charts. And although these still landed broadly within the acoustic/quiet spectrum, in truth any notion of a mass acoustic 'movement' had rapidly fallen by the wayside, in favour of more distinctive sounds.

Loss, Scottish singer-songwriter Colin MacIntyre's 2001 debut as Mull Historical Society, most obviously fits this bill. The result of a childhood spent at the country's margins, MacIntyre's sonic blending of the west coasts of both Scotland and America was an invigoratingly nonconformist broadcast. That same defiance – and the same cottage-industry production method – applies to Thomas and Alex White of The Electric Soft Parade, who demolished and then reconstructed nineties art-rock from their teenage bedroom in Brighton, resulting in 2002's magnificent *Holes in the Wall*. Lowgold's 2001 debut *Just Backward of Square* arrived via more conventional means – one of many records seemingly intended to replicate the success of Coldplay. But the album's lyrics, which traced an inner landscape of uncommon melancholy, marked it out as a similarly unusual offering.

For a kid spending a lot of time in his bedroom by this point, I found all these artists' way of thinking, their lyrics and their methods, both relatable and reassuring. Like many teenagers, I became almost militant about protecting my solitude, while also cultivating an abstract, yet-to-crystallise notion of 'escape' – one that so often aligns itself with the music we consume at that age. Already I was craving the type of distraction that forcing down a can of Heineken in a freezing park while talking about what my friends and I were 'gonna do' on our skateboards[80] couldn't quite provide. During the

[80] Despite our braggadocio, the honest answer was 'next to nothing'.

seemingly endless plateau of those secondary school middle years, this music pointed to a way of coping. If I couldn't *physically* escape (yet), there were at least artists out there who understood a thing or two about suburban frustration. What's more, they had found a way to sing their way out of it.

★★★

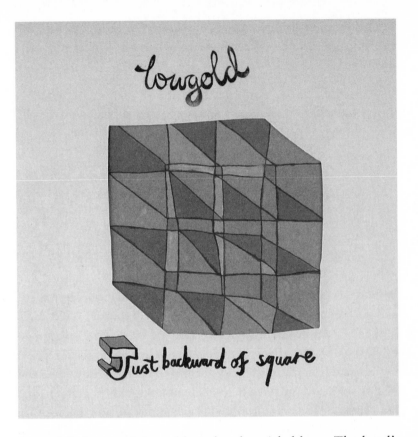

Lowgold's is one of the sadder tales chronicled here. The band's considerable early promise was quickly smothered by a combination of spectacular bad luck and timing; even as early as 2002, just a year after releasing their debut album, they were 'staring down the spectre of bankruptcy', and singer Darren Ford was participating in medical trials at Northwick Park Hospital to make ends meet. Their profile has dwindled, meaning should-be classics 'Beauty Dies Young' and 'In Amber' now languish only in the most dedicated radio researcher's cortex. In a 2008 interview with *Werk.Re*, the interviewer asks Ford where he thinks Lowgold sit in the grand scheme of things. He deadpans 'by the fire exit'. Yet their debut, *Just Backward of Square*, is a modest miracle: a graceful and profoundly melodic collection, which deserves better.

Formed in St Albans in 1997, Lowgold comprised core members Ford, guitarist Dan Symons and bassist Miles Willey. Ford – who had by this point drummed in various bands including The Knievels and Shinecello, and was keen to strike out on his own terms – takes up the story:

> I'd known Miles for a few years before Lowgold happened. We both lived near each other in St Albans, had mutual friends, so it was only a question of time before we met. I played drums in a few different bands during the nineties and ended up playing drums in his for a while. Then we became housemates and it was the natural thing, asking him to play bass when Lowgold took off. I hadn't known Dan long before we started playing together … we met in a student union bar and hit it off straight away. He actually introduced me to the girl who is now my wife the same night. So I got married and found a guitarist in the time it takes to down three drinks.[81]

Ford already had demos of the tracks that would form *The 108 EP*, and with Symons now on board, things fell into place. 'We never spoke for a second about what direction we wanted the songs to go in, how we wanted them to sound. We just let the songs happen. I'd never heard Dan play, had no idea what type of guitarist he was, and he'd never heard my songs before. He just plugged his guitar in and put the headphones on. I pressed play and record, and there it was. There was Lowgold.'[82] The two recorded a demo and sent it off to various labels. Even with such rapid musical chemistry, they must surely have been taken aback at the speed things then began to move.

'We didn't really exist before we got signed. I sent out one cassette copy of the demo I'd finished with Dan, it landed on [A&R man at Nude Records] Ben James's desk, and he called the number scrawled on the tape.' Lowgold didn't even consider themselves an outfit at all until Nude expressed an interest in their demo, as Ford details in an interview with *Crud* in 2001: 'Nude got the demo and asked us, "When's the band next playing?" We said, "Slight problem there, we haven't got a band." So they said, "Here's an idea: why don't you go and actually form a band." So that's what we did.' Knowing he had

---

[81] Author email interview with Darren Ford, October 2019. All quotes taken from this interview unless otherwise stated.
[82] According to the band's bio on the One Little Indian Records website, for a while the band claimed 'Lowgold' was a Nordic word meaning 'of hidden worth'. They later admitted they'd just made it up.

to move quickly, Ford recruited a group to showcase the material, bringing Miles Willey into the fold to play bass – Willey in turn found the band's original drummer, Paul Mayes. 'I think we ran through the songs a couple of times, Ben [James] and Saul [Galpern, founder of Nude] turned up, we played them again, and the next day they offered us a deal. Fucking ridiculous, really.' Lowgold suddenly found themselves sharing a stable with the likes of Britpop agitators Suede and Black Box Recorder.

For Ford, the deal represented vindication after years of work: 'I'd been struggling in bands for years, and all of a sudden Lowgold was falling into place without breaking a sweat.' They headed to Chipping Norton Recording Studios to make their debut album, drafting in Tony Lash on production duties, who had also overseen The Dandy Warhols' *Thirteen Tales from Urban Bohemia* that year. As well as producing, Lash stepped in on drums for much of the session after Paul Mayes departed the project. Unsatisfied with the results they were getting from their neglected surroundings (the studio would close for good later in 1999), they moved to Jacobs Studios in Surrey. Lash continued on drums for these sessions too but, wary that he couldn't tour with them, the band brought in Slowdive drummer Simon Scott as a more concrete replacement. (They went on to record the single 'Counterfeit', which was produced by Dave Eringa, with Scott behind the kit.) The band's debut single, *The 108 EP*, was released in July 2000. Containing 'In Amber', 'Can't Say No', 'The Feelings' and 'God Willing', it was well-liked by the press and awarded 'Single of the Week' in both *NME* and *Melody Maker*. The next single 'Beauty Dies Young' then fared respectably in the charts – skimming the Top 100 at number 67 – and received strong airplay from Steve Lamacq on his Evening Session. The song was remixed for a B-side by one Graham Coxon – an indicator of how quickly the band's star was rising.[83] The band then found themselves on tour with Coldplay, just as the latter were beginning their ascent, and witnessed first-hand the start of the backlash to the New Acoustic Movement – despite it having barely begun. Ford is full of warm praise for his world-conquering contemporaries, however:

[83] It was re-released in 2001, scoring the band their only Top 40 hit.

We like shitting on success in this country. I honestly don't give a flying fuck what anyone thinks about their music, good or bad. The only thing that matters to me is what they were like as people, and they were an absolute dream to tour with. Funny, self-deprecating, generous ... We loved being a tiny part of it, and couldn't be happier for them, all the success that followed.

Lowgold also played with Grandaddy as they toured the UK with *The Sophtware Slump* (2000) – a dream come true for Ford. 'They were my favourite band, so to end up supporting them was a genuine honour. You always worry the people you admire are going to be arseholes in the flesh, but the guys in Grandaddy were wonderful, right down to an atomic level.' With each show they played, Lowgold were gaining momentum. The critical attention was also beginning to snowball: on the eve of their debut – delayed, worryingly, due to ongoing financial troubles at Nude – the band were the subject of a two-page spread in the rarefied territory of *The Sunday Times*'s culture section, who described them as 'spine-tingling ... believe the hype'.

Just Backward of Square was indeed worth the wait. The unusual title, dreamt up by Dan Symons, was inspired by a cricket fielding position: 'It wasn't really a conscious thing to have it sound English and use a phrase that can be taken a number of different ways. A lot of people are saying that we are American sounding. I don't disagree with that – we are very influenced by American bands, so it makes sense to stamp a little bit of nationality on it I suppose.' Accordingly, *Just Backward* evokes a late summer afternoon on the green as the light ebbs away: timeless, melancholic, painted with long shadows. Much as Turin Brakes had attempted on *The Optimist*, the band's sound was an uncannily English twist on American indie stalwarts, containing trace elements of Sparklehorse, Wilco and Dinosaur Jr. This was hardly surprising given Lash's connections to the dark prince of American song, Elliott Smith, for whom he had mixed 1994's *Roman Candle*. Yet for all its transatlantic influences, Lowgold's world was distinctive enough to feel new. Ford recalls recording as a relatively straightforward process, although he admits to having had nerves when recording his first 'big school' vocals on 'Back Here Again':

'Stood in that booth, singing suddenly felt like purposely dropping my guard in a fight.'

Before a word is sung on the album, though, we're given an understanding of its textures and preoccupations. 'Golden Ratio' is a sweet, looping overture, calling to mind the curve formed by the ratio itself. That self-containment is crucial in understanding Lowgold's approach on *Just Backward of Square*. For this, as is made explicit on lead single 'Beauty Dies Young', is an album of making the most of things while they still endure. The chugging guitar and levitating feedback call to mind a becalmed Grandaddy while also serving as the true introduction to Lowgold's stately intentions. *Just Backward* is a classically introspective record, signalled by the recurring mention of internal processes: lungs, circulation and sleep are all frequent touchstones. 'Breathe in mercury / breathe decay' sighs 'Mercury's resigned chorus; 'Just as easy as it flows / as quickly it will leave' warns 'Open the Airwaves'. This is acute and tender songwriting, with the spotlight turned unflinchingly on the self. Nowhere is this more evident than the extraordinary 'In Amber' – one of Lowgold's oldest songs, and the album's most powerful. The anxiety of preservation is again writ large, Ford singing of 'a thread … suspended but not dead'. The mournful 'Never Alone' finds its subject 'in the shade behind the main attraction' – an almost unbearably prescient indicator of where the band would soon find themselves.

After the hype around their early releases, the critical reaction to *Just Backward* was mixed, though the band were not without their champions. Yet it was already becoming clear that, through no fault of their own, Lowgold were not ultimately destined for greatness. Nude were by now pursuing a protracted rescue deal that appeared to be going badly. The band played what proved to be their last public appearance for nearly two years in September 2001, as part of a Tim Buckley tribute night at the Royal Festival Hall. That December, Nude finally collapsed, releasing a statement to the press saying they were 'very sad to announce that it has had no alternative but to go into voluntary liquidation'. This harsh stroke of misfortune meant that Lowgold, just six months after releasing their album, suddenly found themselves in huge debt, without a label and unable to tour.

A post on the band's website, which details their financial woes in forensic and palm-sweating detail, estimates they owed £58,000 between them. 'It fucked me up for a while,' Ford says – and who can blame him. 'Lowgold was everything I'd ever wanted. I'd been dreaming about being in a band since I was six years old. Music was the thing I was supposed to do with my life, so to get the chance to make records, to see our songs in the Top 40 – for a man with zero self-esteem it was an amazing feeling. Then Nude collapsed and it felt like the apocalypse. It didn't help that we ended up fighting bankruptcy for the next two years. That's not what you form a band for.' In addition, the relatively muted public reception that had greeted *Just Backward* meant no one else was willing to take a punt on them; the band's career stalled abruptly, just as it was beginning.

Lowgold began to fragment. Scott departed; Ford, Symons and Willey – who, as partners in the band's company, were liable for the eye-watering debt – began working day jobs, or, in Ford's case, becoming a human guinea pig. They spent six months earning as much as they could, and managed to pay off most of the balance and VAT bills. Still shell-shocked from their experience, and by no means out of the financial woods, they reconvened in Symons's cousin's house in Winnersh, Berkshire in the summer of 2002, where they began laying down demos for their new album. Lowgold's management – which included former Wonder Stuff drummer Martin Gilks – approved of the new material and arranged label showcases for them. It was the first time the band had played together in nearly a year; Gilks filled in on drums. To everyone's relief, they secured a deal with Sanctuary Records, as Symons remembers: 'After everything we'd been through: Nude going belly-up, Simon leaving, the debt, the bankruptcy fiasco ... I really wanted it to be all fanfares and pyrotechnics when we finally signed, but it was more relief than celebration.' It meant that they were finally able to record their second album, after the nightmare that the first had become. The sessions took place in Portland, Oregon, on the tightest of budgets, again with Tony Lash.[84] *Welcome to Winners* (2003), whose title derives from a doctored sign outside Winnersh train station,

---

[84] The band stayed at Lash's house for two months while in Portland to further cut their costs. Miles Willey describes him as 'truly one of our greatest benefactors'.

gathered a clutch of positive responses from critics. *The Sunday Times* continued their fulsome support of the band, calling the album 'another minor masterpiece' in a review that also spoke highly of their debut: '[*Just Backward*] would have been hailed universally as a classic if Lowgold had emerged from Arizona instead of the Home Counties, and had a singer called Hank instead of Darren.' *Welcome to Winners* is indeed another fine record: 'We Don't Have Much Time', 'Let Me Into Yours' and 'Just A Ride' still stand up nicely today, marrying the band's natural knack for melody to more slimmed-down arrangements. Unfortunately, by now it seemed Lowgold had missed the sweet spot of the era, hustled to the sidelines like so many of their contemporaries by louder and perkier propositions. With weary inevitability, they parted ways with Sanctuary after flat sales; the band went their separate ways again.

To his credit, Ford harbours no bitterness about Lowgold's unfairly curtailed career, and he writes with a sanguinity that was always at the heart of his band's vision. Nothing lasts forever. Make the most of what you've got.

> All that's gone now, the anger and frustration. You deal with it and you move on. I'll always be proud of what we achieved. How the fuck could I not be? Yes, it could've gone better. Yes, losing the momentum we'd built up from *Just Backward* was a killer. But those are things we could never have controlled … what we did have control over was the songs we wrote. I still meet people whose lives have been soundtracked in some way by the music we made. Weddings, funerals, heartbreak, falling in love. We were there with them, and that's such a unique privilege. I'll take that.

★★★

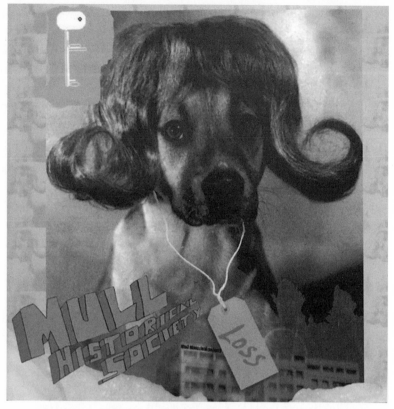

In order to fully understand Mull Historical Society and *Loss* (2001), we first need to get to know a young lad named Colin MacIntyre – who is, to all intents and purposes, the sole member of MHS.[85] 'The Boy in the Bubble', an extended autobiographical essay which appears in the Highlands & Hebrides edition of Wiedenfeld & Nicolson's *Hometown Tales* series of books, is a helpful start. MacIntyre's brilliant account of his Mull childhood begins with a scanned image of a 1984 report card from Tobermory High School. On it, his music teacher writes: 'Colin can get good results but spends too much time showing off to fulfil any potential he may have.' At least they spotted the potential.

MacIntyre is the son of BBC Scotland's widely-respected political journalist Kenny Macintyre,[86] but his two uncles were the first to

[85] It's real, you know. As MacIntyre's project took off, the original Mull Historical Society changed their name to 'The Mull Historical and Archaeological Society' to avoid confusion.
[86] Colin explains that he only took on the capitalised 'I' in the middle of his name because he 'liked the look of it in Primary 7'.

inspire him musically: he remembers them playing Dylan and Beatles songs at a family gathering and, not knowing of either, briefly believed them to be songwriting geniuses. As he recalls:

> I realise that I was actually lucky to have my uncles' covers band wafting across Tobermory to my house from their rehearsals in their plumber's garage. And pretty soon I had access. So I didn't have the conventional inspirations (nor a decent radio signal in these days before universal digital coverage), but I had this treasure trove of plumbing pipes and yes, instruments I could play on and songs I could feel. But even before these more, early teenage years, I had private thoughts that seemed to come with music attached, that I realised were songs, which emerged from 7-8 years onwards … my uncles looked cool and bearded and it wasn't until I was a bit older that I realised these songs they were playing were not their own, they belonged to Bob Dylan, Neil Young and Paul Simon. I was pretty sure those weren't Mull names.[87]

But the most powerful image in 'The Boy in the Bubble', and the most significant for the nascent Mull Historical Society, is of Kenny. Having missed the last ferry back to the island following a week's work on the mainland, he hitches a boat ride with his Uncle Rob, a clam diver. Stormy conditions make the landing too difficult, however, and he is forced to wade ashore, holding aloft his precious cargo: a 1978 USA original Fender Telecaster guitar. As metaphors go, you couldn't wish for a better one: literally the outside world being brought to young Colin, and with it the possibility of both physical and creative freedom. It also represented a big step up for young Colin in terms of his equipment: he had until then been labouring with a red acoustic 'with two holes in it' that he had owned since the age of six. Now doubly armed with a four-track recorder, MacIntyre set about bringing those 'private thoughts' – his own inner world – to life. His teen years were spent writing and recording hundreds of songs, some of which would form the spine of *Loss* – a dense archive he still occasionally draws from today. He also began to spend more time away from Mull, finding inspiration, opportunity

---

[87] Colin was generous enough to answer some questions via email in October 2019, in brilliant detail. All block quotes in this chapter are from that exchange, unless otherwise stated.

and early exposure in Glasgow. He describes how 'the onrush of the populous, of riding buses, trains, having gigs on tap, really inspired me ... the city as much as the island had an influence'. He found a 'home from home' in the shape of Gravity Studios, on Washington Street, where he would go on to record his first two albums.

> I had about 350 songs recorded by the time I got a record deal. I still tap into that well, though a lot of it should stay firmly locked under the bed! But as the songs on *Loss* emerged, I had been demoing in a studio called Gravity, within Berkeley Studios in Glasgow. I had a little demo money from one publisher and recorded 'Barcode Bypass', 'Mull Historical Society' and others. Other publishers kept coming along before I had decided on the right home, and so I had quite a lot of *Loss* already recorded even before I signed with Rough Trade, and subsequently Warner's Blanco y Negro label (and XL Recordings in the US).

Rough Trade opted to release 'Barcode Bypass' as Mull Historical Society's debut single – an unusual but ultimately wise decision. At a sprawling seven minutes, it was hardly snappy or radio-friendly, but there is something about it which beguiles, even now. Unmistakably a storyteller's song, 'Bypass' is an affecting fable about a local shopkeeper whose livelihood is threatened by a new supermarket that 'never sleeps'. It was met rapturously by critics and DJs alike; played in full by Jo Whiley on Radio 1. *Drowned in Sound* described it as a 'tell-everyone-about-this-song masterpiece'. *NME* named it their debut single of 2000. He recalls getting the call from his manager, Tony Beard, who told him the good news: 'I was walking with my grandmother when the call came and the "F- me" words came out of my mouth. My manager said down the phone, "You can't swear in front of your grandmother!" But she was as pleased as I was. I think I knew in that moment that things were going to change ... More than anything, I felt ready for it.' Next on MacIntyre's schedule was his debut album.

There's something strange about featuring this record in a book that celebrates all things acoustic, because *Loss* is a collection whose inspirations lie in electricity and its possibilities: communication, exploration, amplification. In 'The Boy in the Bubble', MacIntyre wonders 'what does it really mean to belong, to *plug in*?' Most immediately it meant that, despite its remote birthplace, *Loss* is hyper-aware of the technologies so distrusted by the New Acoustic Movement: high-speed train lines, public service announcement systems, mass production, supermarkets and junk food. It also contains a handful of truly magnificent pop songs. In short, *Loss* does not contain the whimsical Scottish folk the band name and album title might suggest. *NME*'s review, which describes *Loss* as 'the best acoustic pop album of 2001', also tellingly suggests that 'this should be the album at the end of rock'. They're right: MacIntyre was taking the very idea of the indie band, cutting it into new shapes and carefully decorating the result in time for show-and-tell the next morning. *Loss* felt like an invite to the same kind of private, homemade world the Twisted Nerve cohort were revelling in, with its own rules and distinctive imagery. Most notably in this case, a dog in a wig.

Just as MacIntyre's contemporaries Grandaddy were, brilliantly, on *The Sophtware Slump*, so *Loss* was also concerned with the anxious juxtaposition of technology and nature. But the relationship between progress and tradition is only half the story of *Loss*. It is also directly inspired by a sadder episode in its creator's life: the sudden death of his father in 1999, aged just 54. It meant that even as MacIntyre was beginning to believe Mull Historical Society could be a professional endeavour, he was faced with a devastating personal blow:

> It was a new millennium, and something was in the air, as that year my fortunes seemed to be shifting. My father had died suddenly the year before and 'loss' was very much in my bones I suppose. But [*Loss*] was also a call to action and a tribute in the making to him – it was also about trying to share loss and other feelings, ideas, with others – building a community of some kind.

Kenny's passing also signposted the end of the comparatively idyllic life described in the early pages of 'The Boy in the Bubble'. As his musical skill and reputation grew, Colin increasingly found himself drawn away from the island community he sought to celebrate in his music. That loss, then, is both immediate and personal, but it also refers to one many of us feel: the sudden absence of childhood anchors, of safe harbours. Yet despite its potentially complicating mix of inspirations, *Loss* is a debut album which feels cohesive, testament to MacIntyre's powerful vision for MHS. The idea of building an imaginary community, though it came from a painful place, had obvious resonance. It was a throwback to the childhood dens and clubs of MacIntyre's youth, but it also invested *Loss* with the qualities that every indie fan wants to feel: that they are partaking in something clandestine and privileged. That feeling was augmented by *Loss*'s charmingly wayward artwork – which features glitter, photo collages, a boarding card for the Oban ferry and, most bizarrely, a photo sequence in which a cardboard cut-out of Mull is covered in bath bubbles. Much like Alfie's *If You Happy With You Need Do Nothing*, the visuals reflected the homemade nature of *Loss*'s conception and production. Its arrangements are expansive and varied – a children's choir can be heard on more than one occasion, and a huge range of instruments are listed in the 'players' section of the album's sleeve. Yet there's also a defiantly lo-fi quality to it: 'The album still carried remnants of my old demos – I wanted that texture to it.' MacIntyre cites the scope and ambition of Mercury Rev's *Deserter's Songs* (1998) and Radiohead's *OK Computer* as particularly formative, as well as the eclectic boldness of The Beta Band's *The 3 EPs* (1998) – qualities he would both harness and gently disrupt on *Loss*.

Opening track 'Public Service Announcer' contains the first of many references to broadcasting. 'If this is my public I'm ready for you … Can anyone tell if my stereo's on?', asks the high-speed train driver of the song – but it also sounds like MacIntyre's assertion. After years of seclusion, he was ready to show the wider world his creation; to plug in. The song was based on a poem MacIntyre wrote about 'a disaffected Glasgow transport worker who has music in his head' and drew from his own experience of working in BT's Directory Enquiries department at the time. The exceptional single 'Watching Xanadu' is a gleaming rush of a song which could have been freshly plucked from Phil Spector's back pages.[88] MacIntyre again expresses

---

[88] It also gave MacIntyre the first of his three Top 40 hit singles to date, reaching number 36 in 2002.

his frustration at the limitations of island life: 'find another way to leave'. The formula established on 'Watching Xanadu' – a winning blend of angst and bounce – would become defining features of MacIntyre's later work.

Yet for all its hyperactivity, *Loss* also contains slower songs of real beauty. 'Barcode Bypass', which hardly fits the conventional definition of a ballad – it's more of a laser-scanners-aloft kind of tune, accompanied by a thousand gentle 'bip's – is the strongest. 'Strangeways Inside' is a delicate depiction of romantic love in its oddness and plainness: 'she picks at her teeth / he stares at the cars'. It was the strongest hint at what was to come on subsequent MHS albums, as MacIntyre began to eschew some of his more chaotic production, tending towards a simpler, classic sound. Yet for every moment where *Loss*'s ambitions threaten to overwhelm proceedings, there are ten where a perfect balance is struck. It remains a genuinely exciting and unpredictable listen – an album that could have come out in 1971, 1981, 1991 ... let alone 2001. Which is to say, like loss itself, it is timeless.

Loss was a great success, and Mull Historical Society spent most of 2002 on the road in support of it – memorably playing to 40,000 people at T In The Park in 2002, and joining The Strokes[89] on their UK tour as they continued their lightning-fast rise. (MacIntyre remembers 'electric night after electric night'.) But his personal highlights are those that feel like key narrative developments:

> [I was] standing side of stage [at Oxford Zodiac] waiting to go on, when some bodies were whisked by us into the venue – it was Radiohead. Knowing they were out there as I took the stage was exciting and gave a sense of something coming full circle. As did playing New York for the first time ... and being told David Byrne was there and wanted to say hello. He was one of the first artists I respected, playing 'Road to Nowhere' endlessly on Tobermory football pitch, through what seemed like endless summers.

Although *Loss* was a debut album, it was the closing of a personal chapter for MacIntyre. Another one was about to start: during the

[89] Don't worry, we're getting to them.

recording of the album, he had met the woman who would become his wife. As such, his second MHS collection, *Us* (2003), digs into the tangles and joy of new love with great precision and verve; where *Loss* was concerned with endings, *Us* celebrates discovery. MacIntyre's arrangements are markedly less busy this time around. The bells and whistles that adorned *Loss*, while undeniably charming, had occasionally crowded out the detail of his constructions; on cuts like 'Am I Wrong' and 'Can', his songcraft is clear, without the need for extra glitter. 'Minister for Genetics & Insurance M.P.', which might otherwise have fallen victim to overcomplication, is here given room to breathe: the mix is pared down to little more than a drumbeat and vocal on the verse – when the deft, Flaming Lips-like chorus arrives, with its pretty piano line, it wields the same emotional wallop as an avalanche of multi-tracks. In spite of this refinement, though, it's obvious *Loss* and *Us* are linked. The collage artwork on *Us* echoes its predecessor (the dog in a wig reappears), and even the layout of lyrics on the page is similar. There are also a couple of thematic callbacks to *Loss*: 'The Supermarket Strikes Back' continues the story of 'Barcode Bypass', and the touching '5 More Minutes' is dedicated 'to the living memory of my father' – all of which suggests both albums are part of what we might call the Mull Historical universe. That feeling of consistent artistic vision, of themes emerging and resolving over several albums, is only compounded as MacIntyre brings more music into the world. It's a creative drive that has guided his family for generations, and looks only set to continue.

> I do come from a line of writers on the MacIntyre side of my family ... But the musicians in my family were the island's plumbers. I also consider myself to be just plumbing for songs ... I have worked very hard at my craft too, but yes, my songwriting has always been about telling my story, or placing my story into the hands of characters I observe around me. I just want to keep plumbing for melodies, new stories and most of all not be afraid of the creative cliff. *Loss* and its success is what's made that possible for me.

★★★

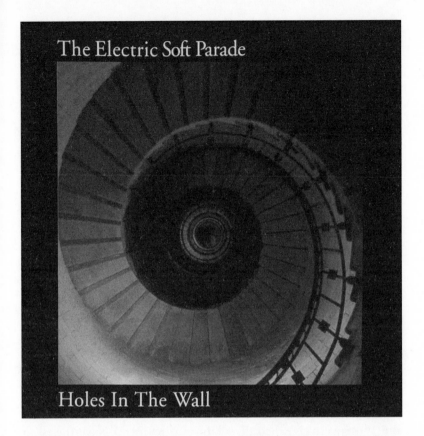

The Electric Soft Parade

Holes In The Wall

I can't write about The Electric Soft Parade without first writing about lamp posts. An odd place to start, perhaps – but the light lamp posts exude, and which illuminates the artwork of the band's early singles, was what first drew me to this endlessly questing music. We all know lamp post light intimately. It renders holy a patch of lonely street on winter evenings; suffuses cold archways with welcoming amber; transforms drizzle into sparks before your eyes. The cover of 2001's 'Empty at the End' did it all: a monochrome photo of the band leaning against a wall on what looks like Chelsea Embankment, lit softly by one of the globular lamps that dot the Thames. To a teenager increasingly curious about stalking my neighbourhood's deserted streets after dinner – my own version of 'escape' – it was impossibly seductive.

That picture, and ESP's other artwork from that era, teasingly suggested everything that was just out of reach to me at the time.

The freedom to wander and be whatever version of 'myself' I was at that point, bound no longer by expectation or curfew. Those liberties were already on their way – but as we all know, nothing can happen quickly enough for a teenager. In the meantime, I snapped up these singles with their classy, glossy finishes, desperate to immerse myself in the comforting gloom they promised. The Electric Soft Parade were one of the first bands about whom I felt a sense of pure discovery. Having heard them once, fleetingly, on the radio, I tracked down their work myself; subscribed to their mailing list; eulogised about them to whoever would listen. For the first time, I was having what I now know to be a familiar feeling for all music obsessives: of getting in on the ground floor; of stewardship and advocacy for something you, personally, have discovered and enjoyed. It was addictive.

Just like the previous two albums in this chapter, *Holes in the Wall* isn't quiet, or even particularly acoustic. Yet The Electric Soft Parade do seem to fit here: they too boasted that inexpressible mix of playfulness, paranoia and deeply felt melancholy that defined the best bands of the period. *Holes in the Wall* is a debut album of rare confidence and no little ambition, from what was at the time a staggeringly young outfit. (Thomas and Alex White were just 17 and 19 respectively when the album was released.) Nevertheless, it set the tone for one of the more interesting and unfairly overlooked musical careers of the last two decades.

The Brighton-based White brothers grew up in a household full of music. Thomas recalls his dad listening to both classical symphonies and more contemporary artists like Elvis Costello and Sparks. Both boys began their trade early: 'Alex started playing piano around the age of four, me not long after, so from an extremely young age we were just totally immersed in learning.'[90] Thomas got serious when he acquired a four-track recorder and began experimenting. 'Once I got my head around the four-track, the possibilities opened up hugely, and I began arranging things in a much more complex and realised way. That was the start of *Holes in The Wall*, really.' The brothers formed a band in their early teens with two school friends, named

---

[90] Interview with Thomas White, July 2019. Subsequent quotes taken from this interview unless otherwise stated.

Fixed Ascent, and later The Feltro Media, at first rehearsing in their bedrooms, then road-testing their material in small venues around Brighton. 'The early shows were great to some degree, but it's easy to see the past through rose-tinted glasses. The reality was probably cacophonous, but spirited and exciting, when we got things right.'

The Feltro Media even went as far as making an album, *The Wonderful World of The Feltro Media* (1999) – a venture undertaken by their management and released on Skye Wreckords in the hope of finding the band a deal. It contained early versions of three songs that would eventually make it onto *Holes in the Wall*: 'There's A Silence', 'Biting the Soles of My Feet', and the title track. Dave Bates's DB Records, which was also in the process of launching Tom McRae's career, signed the band as a two-piece in January 2001. The brothers renamed themselves The Soft Parade,[91] and that year released 'Silent to the Dark' and 'Empty at the End' in April and July respectively. The former was a particularly vivid statement, split into two parts on the original single release: ostensibly a wistful jangle number for its first act, it then stretches over six further minutes of icy piano, beats seemingly comprised of unspooling Sellotape, and burbling, incoherent voices. It was a bewitching early sign of things to come, made even more remarkable because elements of the song were taken from the band's very earliest recordings. 'The verse lead vocal is me, aged about 15, singing into a £15 Maplins mic,' says Thomas. 'Empty at the End' was a more straightforward prospect, bridging the gap between The Feltro Media and this newer, more adventurous undertaking. Its simplicity and radio-friendly chorus meant it received decent radio airplay – recognition which introduced many fresh listeners to this exciting teenage band. They were in for a surprise when the duo's debut album arrived, bursting with experimental vigour.

There's a photo collage in the back of the *Holes in the Wall* CD booklet showing Thomas White's bedroom, where the renamed Electric Soft Parade wrote and rehearsed much of the material on the collection. The walls are crowded with tickets, photographs and drawings – indicative of a band seriously besotted with recorded

[91] A legal challenge from a Doors covers band of the same name prompted them to, ahem, go Electric.

music, both past and present. Clearly visible are posters for three contemporary bands: Suede, Super Furry Animals and Six By Seven – as Thomas says, 'loads of visual stuff and music stuff that totally informed where I was and what I was doing at the time'. Yet in truth the band's influences are almost too numerous to count. Put simply, they wanted to sound like *everyone* – and themselves – at the same time.

In an entertaining interview with the brothers, Mark Beaumont describes a conversation with them as 'like being beaten about the face and body with the entire *NME* back issue cupboard', in a conversation that seems to range over nearly every artist that had released new music that year. The impression is of enthusiastic, unnervingly confident kids, complete with an arsenal of musical references, and the means with which to bend them to their needs. Recalling the sessions for *Holes in the Wall*, Thomas says 'my memory is of just having a huge amount of energy, and good feeling for what we were doing, and just generally feeling extremely wide-eyed and positive about the possibilities of what this mad little record of ours could be'.

With that in mind, it's hardly surprising that *Holes in the Wall* announces itself loudly and rarely lets up. 'Start Again', with its stuttering bursts of guitar and heavily treated vocals, sets the scene for the adventures to come. The two raucous singles, 'Empty at the End' and 'There's A Silence' follow on – the latter is especially robust, boasting a wonderful moment in the final chorus where the guitars lurch, pause… and then freewheel again. Then comes a tender ballad, 'It's Wasting Me Away', which features one of several allusions to windows and curtains: 'There's a line across the window / like the lines across your face'. 'Silent to the Dark' asks us to 'choose between a curtain or a star'. 'You don't get out much / you're hardly locked inside' chides 'Biting the Soles of My Feet'. The imagery is crucial: as suggested by those crowded walls on the artwork, The Electric Soft Parade were making bedroom pop in the most literal sense; investing domestic objects with seismic importance; constructing a lonely inner world bordered by glass, brick and fabric. If staying in had by now become the new going out, *Holes in the Wall* was surely the ultimate soundtrack.

At this point, the album sets off in more psychedelic directions, signposted by the inclusion of the full, nine-minute version of 'Silent to the Dark'.[92] 'This Given Line' amps up the weird even further, as waves of slide guitar in the verse are poleaxed by a driving chorus that could almost have come from a different song altogether. But this pick'n'mix approach to song structure – which came to define the duo's later albums – is best showcased on *Holes in the Wall* by 'Biting the Soles of My Feet'. A delightfully slippery six minutes, it segues between chugging verses, a rushing bridge, and an odd interlude of overlapping vocals repeating 'life goes on'. It's the proggiest moment on the album – yet it also features another one of those choruses that ESP, at their best, do so well: like throwing the bedroom windows open on a new day; like surfacing. 'Biting the Soles of My Feet'[93,] like much of the album's latter half, suggested a band growing up so quickly they had already surpassed the material at the start of the record: bursting with ideas and defying expectations. As it turned out, we hadn't seen anything yet.

Holes in the Wall was met with generally positive reviews, none more so than Jim Wirth's 9/10 verdict in *NME*: 'one of the most impressive debuts of 2002 … they have accidentally transcended all of their idols to come up with a record that redefines British guitar music'. The band were also seriously turning heads on the live circuit, with Dave Simpson awarding their show at Manchester University five stars in a *Guardian* review: 'Britain has not forgotten how to make effortlessly classic, exciting guitar-based pop … If there's a better new British band this year, I'll emigrate to Russia.'[94] *Holes in the Wall* also earned the brothers a nomination for the 2002 Mercury Prize, in a high-quality and eclectic shortlist which hinted at a new vibrancy within British music: debuts from The Coral, Roots Manuva, The Streets and The Bees – as well as Doves, nominated a second time for *The Last Broadcast*. Oh, and David Bowie.[95] In his roundup of the year's nominees for *The Financial Times*, Ludovic Hunter-Tilney

---

[92] This would later be edited down and rereleased as a single – titled, unsurprisingly, 'Silent to the Dark II'.

[93] Which, like 'Silent to the Dark' was cut down to more radio-friendly size and released as 'Same Way, Every Day (Biting the Soles of My Feet)' in 2002.

[94] At time of writing, Simpson remains a British citizen.

[95] The prize was eventually awarded to Ms. Dynamite's magnificent debut, *A Little Deeper*.

described The Electric Soft Parade's sound as 'Highly impressive … their declamatory music conveys a mood of exhilaration and possibility'. They were also awarded 'Best New Act' at the Q Awards, from a shortlist comprising The Bees, The Vines, The Coral and The Cooper Temple Clause. That exhilaration and possibility were about to explode on the duo's second album.

The White brothers followed up *Holes in the Wall* with *The American Adventure,* released in 2003, this time on DB's mother label, BMG.[96] It was a sprawling, stylistically scattershot, yet ultimately rewarding listen. Retaining the most distinctive elements of *Holes in the Wall,* the band then pushed them further – testing themselves almost to breaking point. Says Thomas, 'We just felt we'd done something quite singular and self-explanatory [with *Holes in the Wall*], and the only way to respond to that kind of huge attention on your first record is with a fierce left-turn in every regard.' Thus, the bucking stop-start guitars first seen on 'Start Again' were given renewed purpose on the single 'Things I've Done Before'. The crazy-paving approach to song structure rose again in the form of the many-headed title track. And the brothers' love of a wig-out was given free rein on the beautiful 'Chaos' – perhaps the album's finest moment. Even the artwork on *The American Adventure* felt like a challenge from a band who place great importance on their visual impact: a crude, cartoonish line drawing of three heads, all speaking into the same blacked-out speech bubble, on a plain white background – almost a parody of the digitally altered bust on the cover of Coldplay's *A Rush of Blood to the Head.* You can see and hear the brothers kicking against their status as indie golden boys; retreating further into the bedroom. 'You have to remember I was still just 19 when *The American Adventure* came out, so we were learning as we went,' says Thomas. 'We weren't a band who honed our craft and then went out into the world. We were thrust straight into the centre of it all from the word go.' Somewhat inevitably – given its more experimental, improvised nature – *The American Adventure* was met with mild confusion by press and fans alike, who were presumably expecting a rerun of the poppier moments on *Holes in the Wall.* Yet there were also signs of the

[96] According to Caroline Sullivan's *Guardian* review of *The American Adventure*, the title was inspired by a sign the brothers saw for a Derbyshire theme park.

music press realising they were dealing with songwriters of serious heft: another favourable review described them as 'Frighteningly assured and self-aware … still the Brit siblings to watch'. This sadly wasn't enough for BMG, who dropped the duo after disappointing sales. Undeterred, the band continued to push themselves – and as if ESP wasn't enough, by this time both White brothers were also playing and touring with a successful side project, Brakes, alongside members of British Sea Power.

The Electric Soft Parade, being so young, were among the first musicians to cite influences like Six By Seven and Super Furry Animals in their interviews and their work – a fact that surely represented a symbolic break with the nineties. Their directness also marks them out from some of the NAM. Theirs wasn't a timid, everyman perspective: they were good, and they knew it. And though other projects now jostle for position in the brothers' priorities, The Electric Soft Parade has remained a big part of the Whites' lives. 'I think ESP has remained a going concern over the years because it's family … for the most part we've stayed tight, though we've had our moments. It'd be pretty awkward looking across the table at Christmas going, "Oh, hey! What you been up to this year?" I can't really imagine that.'

Taken together, *Holes in the Wall, Just Backward of Square* and *Loss* suggested intriguing new directions for alternative British music. And while some bands would take up that mantle further down the line, there was only so far an inward journey could take you. By 2002 the popular focus had fallen elsewhere, and introspection was clearly beginning to fall out of fashion – along with the unassuming stars of this book. A fresh generation of music lovers was emerging, undamaged by the excesses of the nineties, and tired of being cooped up. They adopted the rallying cry of a devastatingly smart new group from Glasgow: 'take me out'.

Epilogue

I remember seeing that *NME* new bands feature with
The Strokes, and just thinking: shit.

– Lee Gorton

Unfortunately, the acoustic movement began its demise almost as
soon as it got started. There were traces of the decline even as early
as 2001 (just two years after Travis had released *The Man Who*) and
it was hastened by the emergence, on both sides of the Atlantic,
of an exciting new wave of bands styled by the *NME* as the 'New
Rock Revolution'. Initially led by The Strokes, The White Stripes
and Yeah Yeah Yeahs in the USA, the NRR quickly found its UK
equivalent with the likes of The Libertines, Franz Ferdinand and
Arctic Monkeys.

January 2001, and the release of The Strokes' *The Modern Age EP*,
now looks like an early marker for the end of the acoustic era.
Featuring early versions of 'The Modern Age', 'Last Nite' and
'Barely Legal', it caused an instant sensation, shifting the focus away
from our polite heroes towards these thrift-store raiding New York
private school punks peddling an irresistible update on Television,
New York Dolls and The Velvet Underground. Like Lee Gorton, I
still remember the *NME* cover feature of 9th June 2001 introducing
The Strokes to the UK ('Why New York's Finest Will Change Your
Life – Forever!'). Simultaneously of the past and future, they looked
and sounded like nothing else at the time. As Adam Green succinctly
puts it in *Meet Me in the Bathroom*, Lizzy Goodman's definitive oral
history of New York music between 2000 and 2010, 'The Strokes
seemed to have access to another world.' Their songs were short,
sharp and impossibly catchy. There was simply no denying the likes
of 'Hard to Explain' or 'Someday', however much the old guard
of music critics, who grizzled endlessly about how derivative they
were, tried to kick back. America suddenly looked set to dominate

the musical conversation again: even amid the tragic events of 9/11, and then-Mayor Rudy Giuliani's crackdown on the live music and club scene, New York City was rocking once more. The roster of bands coming out of the area was astonishing; a world away from the relative politeness of the UK scene at the time. There was strength in depth too, with the leading lights augmented by blistering punk-funk and electroclash movements which included James Murphy's LCD Soundsystem, The Rapture, Radio 4 and Fischerspooner. Over the next two or three years, all made their mark, releasing standout singles or strikingly consistent debut albums – and although these artists had hardly emerged from nowhere,[97] their simultaneous cresting had the effect of an electric shock on the rest of the world. It would take the UK a year or two to match their vibrancy.

Forerunners in that regard were The Libertines, led by the *Steptoe and Son*-channelling Pete Doherty and Carl Barât. They released their chaotic debut *Up the Bracket* in October 2002, just over a year after The Strokes' first album *Is This It* had sent UK critics into raptures and squeezed a rare perfect 10 from the *NME*. Now, The Libertines looked set to eclipse Julian Casablancas and co. entirely. Their attractive blend of Albion-worshipping lyrics and clattering musicianship struck a note with a generation of teenagers ready to embrace a reheated punk spirit, and their homegrown status somehow made them more loveable and accessible than their American counterparts. They duly exploded, acquiring a devoted fanbase attracted to their combination of soap-opera spats, magnificent tunes and unrivalled dedication to hedonism at any cost. The Libertines also harked back to Britpop in their amalgamation of potent English nostalgias: namely the tea/twee aesthetic last seen in *Sergeant Pepper's*-era Beatles, and the calculated disorder of *London Calling*-era Clash – both bands with significantly more cultural clout than the Libs ultimately managed. Their time as anything resembling a cohesive unit was inevitably short-lived,[98] yet even as Pete'n'Carl were beginning to break apart following 2004's infuriatingly lax eponymous second album, a rearguard of savvier, more rounded British bands was arriving on the scene.

[97] To borrow a Fischerspooner lyric.
[98] Although it lives on, if you care to brave the vintage military jacket nightmare that is Camden Market on any given Saturday.

Foremost among these were Franz Ferdinand, Bloc Party and Arctic Monkeys. Franz Ferdinand's self-titled debut, also released in 2004, provided a thrilling update on the art rock of the Glasgow School. Not since Orange Juice or Teenage Fanclub had a young Scottish band approached their songwriting with such wit, verve and abandon, and the inescapable 'Take Me Out' quickly became an anthem for a *new* New Wave. Bloc Party arrived just a little later, and their remarkable debut *Silent Alarm* (2005), has arguably fared best in terms of cultural longevity and lasting influence. Kele Okereke's cosmopolitan, emotionally open and precisely performed songs struck something within a generation looking to break away from the braggadocio of the Britpop years, without sacrificing time on the dancefloor in doing so. And Alex Turner's outfit, arguably the most durable of the trio, were terrifyingly young when their pugnacious first single 'I Bet You Look Good on the Dancefloor' hit number one in October 2005. The appearance of the song's video, on what proved to be one of the final episodes of *Top of the Pops*, still lingers in my memory as one of the most exciting things I'd seen for a long time. Refreshingly cheap and nasty-looking, it stood apart from the glut of slickly-produced R'n'B elsewhere on show. Follow-up single 'When the Sun Goes Down' repeated the trick the following January. 2006's debut album, the Alan Sillitoe-referencing *Whatever People Say I Am, That's What I'm Not*, recalled Pulp's glory days – not just geographically, but also in its unflinching portraits of young lust, lies and larks. Increasingly, it seemed that British guitar music had a firm direction again; had pulled sharply into focus after years of metaphorical squinting. Between them, these three bands pointed to an irresistible way ahead.

As this new school of danceable, witty and stylish musicians strutted in and claimed centre stage, it was hardly surprising that acoustic bands weren't getting as much of a look in. 'Last one to the tattoo parlour still likes Turin Brakes,' declared the *NME* in April 2001 – just a month after the release of *The Optimist LP!* – in their review of Black Rebel Motorcycle Club's debut. It seemed to sum up the attitude of the music press, and, by extension, the public. In a rapidly altering cultural landscape, at least a few of these bands were destined to be left behind. The everymen had paid a price: while they undoubtedly fostered a strong connection between listener and artist, it also made them more vulnerable to being usurped by slicker, more stylised propositions. It also meant that when criticism inevitably arrived, it felt more personal and wounding. It's no coincidence that many of these acts have struggled with the effects of fame – in many cases, they simply weren't expecting it.

Yet the profits reaped by the everyman aesthetic didn't go unnoticed by record labels. In fact, many set about trying to replicate the 'just an ordinary bloke who happens to write classic songs' formula, established by David Gray and Coldplay, over the next decade. The most potent of these incarnations today is Ed Sheeran – it's now impossible to listen to commercial radio without hearing a project that he has either fronted, written, or exerted some influence over. As Alex Petridis notes in his 2019 *Guardian* article on the rise of 'boring pop' – which also includes the likes of Lewis Capaldi, George Ezra, Adele and Jess Glynne – 'here was ordinariness, not as a sniffy reaction to pop's excesses but as a saleable commodity in itself'. This was the logical extension of the everyman's popularity; emerging talent could now simply be dressed down in scruffy jeans and an artfully mussed haircut, then sold back to the masses as a voice of the people. The stratospheric success of the latest in this line, Lewis Capaldi, suggests it is still working.

A feeling of millennial acceleration attended the nut-and-bolts side of the music world at this time, too. The improvement of home studio and file-sharing technology hadn't just made music easier to produce: it also meant bands were now able to bypass much of the traditional rigmarole of the industry.[99] And although social media was still in its infancy, we were also starting to see the dawn of a new type of artist, one that interacted freely with their fans, shared new music for download as soon as it became available – in short, one that was more *present* than ever before. The gap between performer and public had become narrower; a relationship that was now more of a

[99] When I interviewed Turin Brakes, Gale Paridjanian told me a story from the turn of the century that sums up how quickly things have moved on. While staying in a remote Italian village, the band received a call from their label asking them to approve one of their videos for release. A VHS copy was couriered to them, and they had to travel with it to the next village along – the only place available where there was a video player – watch it through, and then phone through their verdict. It's a process that would have taken mere minutes in 2020 – back then, it took a whole day.

conversation than a broadcast. Suddenly, nineties bands were being outpaced and outflanked, left spinning by shrewder and more flexible competition. The idea of a traditional website was already becoming irrelevant – many of the acts I interviewed confessed to having one without really knowing the point of it. The *real* progress was being made elsewhere: the apparently unstoppable rise of Facebook, YouTube and Twitter in the mid-noughties meant that, if one's presence wasn't strongly felt on those outlets, you effectively became invisible. For bands used to at least *some* artistic distance – writing, recording, touring, doing a round of interviews and beginning the cycle again – the idea of being always 'on' must have come as a shock. It was difficult to escape the impression that the more traditional acts were being overtaken on every side.

All of which is not to say that acoustic/quiet music stopped altogether. Far from it: José González's starkly beautiful *Veneer* (2005), Fionn Regan's lyrical acrobatics on *The End of History* (2006), and Bon Iver's aching postcard from isolation, *For Emma, Forever Ago* (2007) all kept the flame alive. Yet these albums now felt like genuine outliers; they didn't link up to a wider ideal, as it sometimes felt like our acoustic bands had done. Despite their individual brilliance, they were just that – statements from brilliant individuals. But then, by the mid-2000s, the idea of *any* homogenised musical or cultural movement was beginning to fragment. In his wise, prescient conclusion to *1996 & The End of History*, David Stubbs attributes this splintering of collective cultural moments to 'The collapse of central agencies over the last twenty years … in 1996 there was a *Top of the Pops*; now there is not. In 1996 there was a *Smash Hits*; now there is not … The nineties were the last decade whose numerical description evoked a raft of political, cultural and stylistic signifiers, as if they were all of the same piece.' That collapse carries through to the social element of pop culture 'movements' too, with Stubbs concluding that 'future political activity … will be decoupled from pop-cultural upheavals'.

The largely apolitical nature of the New Rock Revolution summed up this 'decoupling' perfectly. Where Britpop had been fused – however awkwardly – to a swelling social cause, New Rock and the protests it soundtracked were essentially incompatible. So while it was clearly more vibrant than the NAM, the NRR soon felt like just another attempt to force a Britpop-type moment into a world where one could no longer realistically exist. As a result, many of the New Rock bands ended up having more intense careers than their acoustic predecessors – but they burned out far quicker. In this case, slow and steady appears to have won the race, with many of the original New Rock acts now trading on dubiously won heritage status barely a decade after their original success.

There was a growing sense throughout the noughties that the future of music lay with dazzling and outlandish one-offs – and away from guitars. UK Garage had exploded in parallel to the acoustic movement, providing a fresh and innovative riposte to the R'n'B being produced Stateside at the time. Post-2003, the sound evolved again, and now the leading British artists in grime, hip-hop and pop suddenly sounded a lot more exciting than four guys named 'The Somethings'. These acts transcended their respective stables as a result, achieving mainstream success in a manner that often recalled the early years of punk.[100] Dizzee Rascal's win at the 2003 Mercury Music Prize, for his frenetically exciting debut album *Boy in Da Corner*, seemed especially symbolic – seismic confirmation that the old guard was finally being challenged. As Dan Hancox writes in *Inner City Pressure*, his fascinating history of grime, 'Beneath the headlines about this remarkable teenage prodigy, there was a partial recognition that something else was going on … an underground scene underneath the breakout star.' It was clear a new era was beginning – although it would prove to be more chaotic, multi-layered and confusingly disparate than anything that had gone before it.

Let's rewind all the way back to the *Thirty-Nine Steps*-referencing video for 'Writing to Reach You'. As Fran Healy dodges aircraft fire while running across a frozen field, it's striking as an image that, in retrospect, makes a perfect metaphor for the fickle critical perception towards Travis and their contemporaries. Many of these bands fell

---

[100] In recent years, grime has also established itself as the foremost vehicle for political dissent, just as punk did in the 1970s: witness Stormzy and Dave's respective appearances at the 2018 and 2020 Brit Awards, during which they heavily criticised successive Conservative Prime Ministers Theresa May and Boris Johnson.

victim to a careless and fad-chasing music industry looking for the next big thing, who turned on them with equal vigour as soon as something shinier came along. Yet as we've seen, the vast majority of the acts featured here still command critical and public admiration; their music still exerts a hold on those that encountered it. It certainly does on me. Is it time to think more kindly about these acoustic records, to acknowledge that they *did* and maybe even still *do* mean something more to us? If so, what does that acknowledgement look like? There's no easy answer, but I'd like to think it goes beyond a simple anniversary show or album play-through; so many of these artists are still out there, giving us more than their past. You may think of some of them as heritage acts by now – but *they* certainly don't.

Without getting too philosophical, it's also worth considering the purpose of music itself here. Great art should obviously agitate, challenge and innovate – but there's no denying that it can also comfort, soothe and mollify. Is that not an equally valid way to appreciate it? This is an invitation to embrace the so-called 'average' without fear of compromising some carefully honed notion of taste or reputation. If there is joy to be found in this music, why should it matter how cool it is?

More than anything, though, it turns out this book is a parable about the random nature of success. I find the contrast between Coldplay and Lowgold's respective stories particularly powerful. Former tour-mates, the bands' lives have since gone in completely different directions, but both seem content with their lot. Darren Ford's sanguine perspective of Lowgold's fate seems to sum up the generous spirit of the era. That's not to suggest it was devoid of passion or fire; there's a strain of fervent advocacy here, too. In Kings of Convenience and their brand of radical stillness. In Kathryn Williams and her determination to help women achieve equality in the industry. In The Electric Soft Parade, keeping on at a project even after the spotlight has moved on, for the sake of joy and of family. The six-year window of 1998-2003, so often skipped over when we tell the story of British music, ultimately gave us a set of artists who valued kindness, vulnerability and community – and delivered those principles in the form of varied, ambitious and frequently extraordinary music. And while taken together they only form the slipperiest of musical 'movements', they are bound together through what they stood for. We should cherish them.

Appendix; or what they did next

Travis

Today, Travis are rightly viewed with enormous affection. Recent shows celebrating the 20th anniversary of *The Man Who* (along with a reissue of the album, and a physical release for that 1999 Glastonbury show) have been warmly received. I emailed Fran Healy to ask about what he remembers from the height of *The Man Who*'s success. 'The workload was overwhelming, so there was no point along the way where I could smell the roses. It hit me about two years later, when we stopped – I was walking down Oxford Street and people were looking and whispering to their companion "There's that guy from Travis." I could only make out the "sss" of Travis though. It was weird.' What advice would he give the young Fran now? 'I would let him get on with it. Wisdom gained by experience has a habit of cutting off the paths less travelled, and the paths less travelled is where all the interesting stuff lies.'

In 2018, Healy revealed to *NME* the despondency he felt at the critical reception to *The Man Who* immediately after the album's release, and the subsequent joy at its eventual victories. 'Everyone was very depressed, especially when the reviews came out for it … but it soared … good records will always be good records, shit records will always be shit records. You can't ever change that. The job of your band is to be proud of what you've done.' They can be proud – and could even claim (somewhat reluctantly, perhaps) to be the sentinels of a new musical movement.

David Gray

Gray's most recent album *Gold in a Brass Age* (2019) found him delving deeper into the electronic side of his sound, still adding slowly to his own sonic language. In an interview with *PopMatters* in support of that year's tour, he details his mindset while writing, and concludes: 'These days, I'm looking for any new way to come back into music from a different angle.' That's an admirable stance for a songwriter who could easily have relaxed following the singular accomplishments of *White Ladder*.

In August 2019, following the *Gold in a Brass Age* tour, Gray returned to his childhood home of Solva to rest, tweeting 'Greetings from Sunny Solva. Back home in West Wales and visiting some of my old haunts. If there's a more beautiful place on planet Earth, I'm yet to find it.' It's been a long and strange voyage for Gray – one he is still on, and one that few of us will ever take.

Dido

Dido's decision not to tour the material around *Safe Trip Home* (2008) and *Girl Who Got Away* (2013) meant those albums were inevitably low-key in comparison to the enormous impact of her early work. These days, she is ready to return to the fold. A new album in 2019, *Still on my Mind*, which leant further into her association with electronica, pushed her sound still further away from those early signature singles. Again, comparisons with David Gray are valid; both artists have achieved commercially at the highest level – and are now happy to experiment, knowing that each new iteration will be greeted by loyal fans. As she embarked on a substantial tour for the first time in over a decade, she spoke to the *i* newspaper: 'I'm genuinely looking forward to seeing people at gigs. As a songwriter there's only so long I can go without that communication, that magic that you have on stage.' In a typically self-deprecating moment, she describes asking her Twitter followers what they would like to hear at the upcoming shows: 'So many songs from the third album [*Safe Trip Home*] come up. I thought no one heard it.' That combination of grounded perspective and inherent knack for melody, which has so defined her career, appears undimmed.

Doves

Doves continued their run of exemplary singles in 2005 with what would become one of their best-loved songs, 'Black and White Town'. Third album *Some Cities*, also released that year, marked a further evolution in the band's sound, boasting a more direct and less baroque palette than *The Last Broadcast*. Yet it seemed Doves were beginning to get weary: the effects of two decades of writing and touring had started to weaken the band's resolve, even as they hit their commercial peak. That imperceptible sag informed Doves' fourth collection, the fraught and sometimes unfocused *Kingdom of Rust* (2008): 'There was some personal stuff going on at the time … we really struggled with that record,' says Andy Williams. And even though *Kingdom of Rust* has its moments, not least the imperious title track, the announcement of a hiatus carried with it a palpable sense of relief. For the first time since the early nineties the band fragmented, with the Williams brothers forming Black Rivers in 2014, and Goodwin releasing a solo album, *Odludek*, in the same year.

2019 saw the band reunite and tour, with a handful of headline dates and a support slot for Noel Gallagher – and in 2020 a fine new album, *The Universal Want*, saw the band recapture former glories, reaching number one in September.

Elbow

Given Elbow's now-ubiquitous presence in the nation's living rooms and car radios, it's odd to think it was actually Doves who were more successful in their early years, having scored two number one albums – with *The Last Broadcast* and *Some Cities* – by 2005. However, the 2008 release and subsequent Mercury Music Prize triumph for Elbow's imperious *The Seldom Seen Kid,* and its inescapable lead single 'One Day Like This', saw the balance tip firmly in their favour. They have been in the ascendancy ever since, securing a trio of number one albums themselves, with *The Take Off and Landing of Everything* (2014), *Little Fictions* (2017) and *Giants of All Sizes* (2019).

Predictably, my own favourite Elbow song, 'Lippy Kids', is one that speaks most clearly to my teenage self – the teenager I was when I met Garvey back in 2002. Even a decade later, on his fifth studio album with Elbow (2011's excellent *Build a Rocket Boys!*), he can dig unerringly to the centre of adolescent experience. 'Nobody knew me at home anymore', he sings – so perfectly communicating the feeling of dislocation which arrives like a sudden storm, to so many. If this is the sound of somebody outgrowing their hometown, it is exit music of the sweetest kind. One gets the feeling Garvey has never truly left. Maybe I haven't, either.

Damon Gough's Springsteen influence crystallised on his fifth album, *Born in the U.K.* (2006) – an often valiant attempt to parse The Boss's maximalist production and gritty lyricism with Gough's own experiences of the English north. Yet even though he still appeared to be finding inspiration, *Born in the U.K.* also confirmed there was no going back to the lo-fi Boy of old. His quick ascent to the top, which saw him shrug off the murkiness of his early efforts, had also seemingly stripped him of something fundamental to the Badly Drawn Boy aesthetic.

Three years passed, punctuated only by the release of *Is There Nothing We Could Do?* (2009), the stately soundtrack to the TV film *The Fattest Man in Britain*. More troublingly, Gough was beginning to cut a frustrated figure on stage: two unfortunate minor incidents, in Los Angeles in 2010 and Northampton in 2012, saw him give as good as he got from hecklers before walking off – he announced a three-month break from touring after the latter. In a *Guardian* interview to promote the *Bewilderbeast* 15th anniversary shows in 2015, he told Luke Bainbridge, 'I'd like to apologise now to anyone who reads this who was at that Northampton gig … I'd love to go back there and do another gig and make amends, if they'd have me back.' Looking back at the work he was touring at the time, it's little wonder Gough was frustrated with the technical difficulties, because it remains some of his strongest. Despite its awkward title, 2010's *It's What I'm Thinking Pt.1: Photographing Snowflakes* contains some beauties, including the single 'Too Many Miracles', which already feels like a lost classic. 'Hasn't it been a strange old year?', he asks – and so it would prove to be.

But this is a story with a happy ending. Those recent *Bewilderbeast* shows, and the making of a brilliant 2018 documentary about the record, seem to have galvanised Gough. You still get the sense there is more to come from him. In that same interview he expresses a wish to 'release another 10 albums in the next 15 years' – and you don't doubt he will. The prospect of a happier, more settled Badly Drawn Boy is one to savour, and a new album in 2020, *Banana Skin Shoes*, saw Gough return to some of the playful experiments of old. When it comes to this most elusive and unpredictable of artists, there is always the chance of finding another pearl.

Alfie

Nowadays, Lee Gorton is a picture of contentment – able to listen back to his band's efforts with a degree of fondness, and describing how his young daughter, Isabelle, has tweaked the words to Alfie's 'Isobel' to the far more accurate 'Isabelle My Name'. He now works as a rep for a craft ale company, which he jokingly describes as 'the new rock'n'roll'. And although there are no plans to return to music any time soon, he now reflects on his career with pride: 'One thing I always understood – the most moving part of it all – our fans, the ones I met were the loveliest people – we drew lovely people towards us with our music. They were wonderful, they were with us. I still can't believe we made it happen.'

Coldplay

Coldplay's third album, *X&Y* (2005), refined the band's formula further, and though not as consistent as *A Rush of Blood to the Head*, it contained possibly the most potent distillation of their sound to date in the anthemic 'Fix You', which went on to become one of their biggest hits. The final hidden song, the beautifully tender 'Til Kingdom Come', was famously written for Johnny Cash – sadly the great man died before he had a chance to record it. 'Til Kingdom Come' lent an air of finality about *X&Y* that was perhaps unintentional; it was also a goodbye to the acoustic side of the band.

After a three-year break, a refreshed and sonically reconfigured Coldplay kicked on again with the euphoric, string-led 'Viva La Vida', which belatedly scored them their first number one single. The album of the same name, released in 2008, took them in an even poppier direction, and saw their audience sizes swell still further. At the same time, Martin's preoccupation with Coldplay's visual identity became more cohesive and (literally) uniform, as the band began a period of dressing in customized military garb. Then, in typically ambitious fashion, they ramped up the impact once more for 2011's *Mylo Xyloto* – this time favouring an exuberant, technicolour splatter of graffiti and neon. Their evolution from diffident, sloppy college band to hyper-styled rock royalty was complete.

The release of *Eyes Open* (2006) saw Snow Patrol consolidate their place in the rock chronicles. It was unashamedly an album of arena-ready songs – and was also the first Snow Patrol album to be played exclusively in those venues. Where *Final Straw* had been a high-stakes gamble from Gary Lightbody (who had 'just assumed I'd be a rock'n'roll star' after their first album), the band's fourth record oozed confidence, showcasing Snow Patrol fully at ease with their gear change. *Eyes Open* gave the band their first number one LP, and continued a remarkable run – begun by *Final Straw* – that has seen them score six Top Three albums in a row, including *Up to Now*, their best-of-so-far compilation album. Snow Patrol's star rose even further, with the breakout success of 'Chasing Cars' opening doors for the band that Lightbody must only have ever dreamed about. Having duetted with Martha Wainwright on the superb 'Set Fire to the Third Bar' (a single from *Eyes Open*), he continued collaborating, working with talents as diverse as Ray Davies (covering 'Tired of Waiting for You' on 2010's *See My Friends*) and Taylor Swift (on 'The Last Time', a co-write with Jacknife Lee for 2013's *Red*).

Yet it seems all was not well for Lightbody, as a long-time sufferer of anxiety and depression. Having always tended to the heavy side of alcohol consumption (he has two replacement teeth in his lower jaw, the result of a fall outside a club in Glasgow in the early Snow Patrol days), he began drinking more regularly to cope with the band's rapid ascent, and the worries that often attend such developments. Despite achieving everything he could have wanted, he records feeling 'incapacitated' by ongoing problems with his mental health. In an interview to promote Snow Patrol's 2018 album *Wildness*, he opened up to *The Scotsman* about what he carefully never calls a dependence, but does concede he was 'drinking for Ireland ... It was pretty much built-in. I couldn't think about a day without it, think about another way to be, because it seemed to insulate me against what I was feeling.' He had decided to quit drinking altogether in 2016, after a series of infections in his ears, eyes and sinuses. These days, he cuts a less troubled figure – and is also sanguine about his band's frustrating early years, telling the *Belfast Telegraph* in 2018:

I thought we were going to be big from the start – and then when we weren't, I started thinking, 'Maybe this is never going to happen' … I had too much ego at the beginning. Over time, that gets drilled out of you. Looking back, I'm grateful that we were allowed a gestation period because I think I'd have been absolutely insufferable. I wanted too much at the beginning – I wanted world domination. I don't think I was over-confident and I certainly wasn't cool. It was more like I was charged with this energy that was probably no real use to me.

As the band look back on a glittering and varied twenty-five years, it seems telling that their latest project (2019's *Reworked*) is an album of rearranged Snow Patrol classics. It feels like Lightbody giving himself a second chance to simply enjoy his own band's music, unburdened this time by his ghosts.

Kings of Convenience
Following *Unrest*, Erlend Øye continued effectively as a solo artist, starting his Whitest Boy Alive project in 2003 while living in Berlin. That collective released two albums, *Dreams* in 2006 and *Rules* in 2009, both of which met critical acclaim. Two Kings of Convenience albums have followed since *Quiet is the New Loud*: 2004's *Riot on an Empty Street*, which features two tracks with Leslie Feist, the charming duet 'Know-How', and closer 'The Build-Up'. *Riot* saw the pair audibly absorbing further influence from jazz and bossa nova, and is overall a livelier affair than *Quiet is the New Loud*. The highlight of these excursions is the single 'I'd Rather Dance With You', which matches a snappy piano line with a tale of meeting someone at a house party – laced with their customary lyrical self-doubt ('I doubt my reply would be interesting for you to hear'). It represented a broadening of sonic horizons that echoed the pair's own expanding world view. Arguably their career-high album is also their most recent: 2009's *Declaration of Dependence*, which *Pitchfork* called 'the best new full-length of its style you'll hear this year'.

Bøe still lives in Bergen, where he writes and lectures on urbanism and architecture from a psychological perspective – as he puts it, 'To spread the idea that humans need to live in humane environments.' Erlend Øye has settled in the Sicilian town of Siracusa – most recently releasing an Italian-language album, *Legao*, in 2014. Unusually for such a well-loved band, the pair see comparatively little of each other, only coming together to work on new music. And what of the band's legacy, as they approach a third decade of craftsmanship? 'I'm immodest enough to say that our *Quiet is the New Loud* project wasn't just a musical trend,' says Eirik, 'but a broader cultural project. In many ways we're losing badly, but I'll still fight for the idea that writing and recording should be simple and natural. Human beings have created technology, but we are most happy when we're surrounded by things that remind us that we are human.'

Turin Brakes

It's fair to say that by 2005, and third album *Jackinabox*, times had changed both for Turin Brakes and the wider world. Yet the band's popularity has endured. *Jackinabox* nudged into the Top Ten and spawned another crop of laudable singles. It's a pattern that continues to this day. Turin Brakes have fallen from favour with the cooler music magazines, yet with each subsequent release they add to their impressive portfolio of favourable broadsheet reviews, and continue to reward their loyal fanbase with a dynamic live show. 'It comes down to value in the end,' says Olly Knights. 'People know they are going to get the best we can give them, and there's so much dynamic material across eight albums that the show has a great depth. It feels like albums are just companion pieces now, rather than the main focus for fans – but we still put in as much of ourselves as when we made *The Optimist LP*.'

The duo are still dedicated to the art of songwriting – they now help younger singers to break through, drawing on their two decades of creative experience. They also remain thoroughly amiable company. For my final question I ask them if, in hindsight, they would have done anything differently at the time of *The Optimist*. 'Probably I would drink a lot less and walk a lot more,' quips Gale, while Olly says: 'I think that debut is as pure as it will ever be for us … with success you lose that. Then it becomes about finding new ways to get back to that old beginner's mindset. But I'm fine with that – it's all way better than having a real job.'

Kathryn Williams

Kathryn Williams followed up *Little Black Numbers* the following year with *Old Low Light* (2002), consolidating her reputation as one of the most consistent and melodic songwriters of the period. She continues to make work of enviable consistency and clarity. 2015's remarkable *Hypoxia*, created in response to the fiftieth birthday of Sylvia Plath's *The Bell Jar*, received an especially warm critical reception: 'Plath's work and life has impacted on songwriters for many years ... but there are very few who, like Williams, seem to have come to some greater understanding of the novel other than it being a handy cipher for ennui-infected teenage girls.'

Williams has never lost her love for visual art, often producing prints to accompany her sung work. The songwriting workshops with Chris Difford have also proved a hit. 'For weeks [before the first session] I was like "What am I going to do, what I am going to teach?" I'm not a teacher, and I never got lessons, but once I'd done the week, I understood exactly what it was about. It's not about teaching people to write songs – it's not *school*, it's just about creating a really great space so people can spend a week of their lives making music.' One of the most rewarding elements, she says, is working with writers 'who have been really difficult at the beginning of the week, a pain in the arse, and then you realise it's just because they're scared – and then they love it, and go home with five or six songs and loads of friends. You've actually changed their lives – and it's nothing to do with songwriting at all.'

Lowgold

Rapidly becoming disillusioned with the music industry, Lowgold formed their own label, DedTed Records, in 2005. On it, they released a double album of B-sides, rarities and live tracks from the *Just Backward* era, knowingly titled *Keep Music Miserable*. Dan Symons sums up the mood at the time: 'That, as far as we were concerned, was the end of it ... there was no particular reason to keep being in the band.'

The most recent evidence of Lowgold as a unit can be found with the biographies and reintroductions produced for their seemingly final 2008 album, *Promise Lands*. They strike a suitably sombre note: 'The trio know what it's like to look up and see a storm gathering: since releasing their debut album ... they have faced the heaviest of weather.' This was a reference not only to their plagued career, but also to a significant event within team Lowgold – the death of Martin Gilks in 2006. Reuniting to play at his funeral, Ford revealed he was sitting on a tranche of songs that could be shaped into a record. They decided to give it one last shot and recorded the collection in ten days. Despite understandably being 'clouded with loss', *Promise Lands* is musically the brightest of Lowgold's records. Gone, for the most part, are the crunchy guitars and close-mic'd vocals, replaced by a clean, clear sound. It sounds like a band writing for themselves, as indeed Ford was, since none of these 'intensely personal' songs were really intended to make it out into the world. That they did is something to celebrate.

> *Promise Lands* is the album I'm most proud of. We hadn't really seen or spoken with each other for months leading up to it, we were only a band in name by that point. We'd had the shit kicked out of us pretty much since Nude imploded ... Then Martin was killed in a motorbike accident in 2006. It was utterly devastating. He was so important to everything we'd done as a band and even more important to us as a friend... Martin felt like part of the band. Losing him could've marked the end for us, but it had the opposite effect. I'd kept writing even though the band was falling apart in slow motion, and had 20-odd songs finished ... Martin dying brought the three of us back together. I played the demos I'd recorded to Miles and Dan, we all got excited about music again then one thing led to another and we decided to start our own label, put a record out ourselves ... I'm so proud of what we did, all of it, every album. But getting *Promise Lands* out felt like a genuine victory. I'm glad we had something positive and beautiful to dedicate to Martin.

Post-*Promise Lands*, ten years have passed with no official word from the band. And while others from their era have gone on to far greater heights – or stepped away for a while, only to revisit their legacies – Lowgold have drawn a firm line under their musical endeavours. And who can blame them? Yet the sense of missed opportunity when revisiting *Just Backward of Square* is palpable; under different circumstances, they might have been as enormous as their debut album suggested. Sadly, we'll never know how high they could have flown.

Mull Historical Society

Mull Historical Society's third album *This Is Hope* (2005) saw Colin MacIntyre further stripping back his sonic palette after a trip through the American south listening to David Bowie's *Low*, Television's *Marquee Moon* and Lou Reed's *Transformer*. 'Those three albums taught me that less is more – I have a tendency to throw a lot into a song and you don't always need so much,' he says in an interview in 2004. That self-awareness has served him well since: recognising a need to sidestep the MHS project for a time, he released two solo albums under his own name: *The Water* in 2007, and *Island* in 2009. Recent years have seen a return to Mull Historical Society, as well as a writing career: he released debut novel *The Letters of Ivor Punch* in 2015. Set on Mull, it went on to win Edinburgh International Book Festival's First Book Award. And with a charming children's picture book under his belt now, too (*The Humdrum Drum*, Little Door, 2018), the Society looks as strong as ever. In recent years he has been working on an electro-pop project called Field Stars, and has adapted *Ivor Punch* for the stage.

The Electric Soft Parade

The Electric Soft Parade followed up *The American Adventure* with the excellent *Human Body EP* in 2005, which contains their finest moment to date: the brilliant, McCartney-esque 'Cold World'. That collection laid the groundwork for 2007's *No Need To Be Downhearted*, whose lead single 'If That's the Case, Then I Don't Know' was praised for its 'octopus-on-crack drumming … this could be the feelgood hit of the summer'. It was the sound of The Electric Soft Parade belatedly throwing off the shackles of expectation and cutting loose, and it sounded magnificent. 'You'll never know the world from inside', on 'Life in the Back Seat' felt like a further rallying call. Once again, the artwork for *No Need* said everything: the bright sunny day, the child-like landscape, the colourful buildings – a world away from those dimly lamplit early singles. *No Need* set The Electric Soft Parade on the path they still find themselves on, with 2013's self-released *Idiots* one of the most satisfying summations of their sound yet.

After resting the ESP moniker for several years, the brothers released a new album, *Stages*, in January 2020. It's a record primarily about grief, but it also finds Alex and Thomas pushing their sound further again, stretching their songcraft over structures that rarely dip below the seven-minute mark. The vibrancy of their ideas appears inexhaustible.

Me

After my voice broke almost overnight in my early teens (on the same holiday I met Guy Garvey, as it happens), it soon became painfully clear that it had gone too far in the other direction, settling on a low drawl only suited for libraries. Almost immediately, my promising career in am-dram went down the pan, and I began to mumble where before I had sung. One of my university lecturers would later describe my unfortunate output as 'subsonic' in front of a class of my peers. I struggled to make myself heard in bars and clubs as I navigated adolescence, feeling like I was shouting just to reach the level others achieved seemingly without effort, my heart sinking each time a group leaned in to listen. My parents, hardly loudmouths themselves, seemed to provide genetic evidence that the situation would not improve.

My father, while never truly well, finally stopped deteriorating at such an alarming rate after a few agonising years. We learned there was no pattern, no recovery and no let-up to his illness, but we managed. Our house underwent a transformation, converted to accommodate wheelchair use. And while my sister and I struggled with the effects of seeing our parents so reduced, our family began to adjust to this drastically altered normality. Throughout this period, music was a constant source of solace, and although the NAM would always have a special place in my heart, I too fell for the New Rock Revolution.

For a brief, weird moment I became an unlikely tastemaker at school. (Among my lot, anyway. God knows what the popular kids were up to.) Fervent discussions of the nascent scenes in New York and London attended many lessons and lunch breaks – or at least, what I could glean of them from my well-to-do Westcountry outpost. New CDs were swapped among our growing cabal of music lovers like football stickers. I was still hopelessly off the pace when it came to attracting the opposite sex, but my relative musical expertise became a way of ensuring a *little* bit of attention came my way. Repetitive bus journeys to and from school were brightened by cautiously intimate headphone-sharing moments, and the minor satisfaction of having brightened up a girl's day with a new song was enough to reassure me I might not be entirely repellent. Ever guided by my trusty *NME*, and by now in full thrall to the New York scene, I diligently gathered imported DFA samplers; pored over their full-page feature breaking down every second of Electric Six's 'Danger! High Voltage'; even believed them when they wrote that terrifying one-hit wonders A.R.E. Weapons were going to be the next big thing. Through all of this, bigger thoughts were stirring. Not only was I was starting to realise my love for introducing people to music, I was re-finding a place for myself in the world.

Much as Nirvana had spent their career pointing fans to bands like The Vaselines and Teenage Fanclub, so the New Rock bands – particularly The Strokes – became my influencers. Guided By Voices, another band who ended up shaping my own burgeoning musical identity, first appeared on my radar thanks to Julian Casablancas's recommendations.[101] Then came another pivotal moment in my listening career: a bright new music shop, Fopp, opened up in Bath's Corridor. Inside lay treasures that a musically curious teenager like me could only dream of, including reasonably priced CD versions of – well, just about everything. I duly became a scholar of popular music history, ploughing through The Beatles, Dylan, Springsteen and Talking Heads at an electric pace. Then something *else* clicked, and suddenly no genre was out of bounds – I dipped my toes into hip-hop, electronica, country, drum'n'bass, soul, reggae and whatever 'world' music I could get my hands on. Quickly, my early musical obsessions, wrapped up in their tastefully muted artworks, began to

---

[101] In 2001, the bands even played two nights together, December 30th and 31st, at Harlem's Apollo Theater. I imagine some beer was consumed.

seem less vibrant. I listened to them less and less as time went on, becoming as detached from them as I eventually did from my old school friends. Yet something always drew me back – and it always will.

My tentative early experiences of live music included a vomit-spattered Libertines gig at Bristol's Colston Hall (now the Bristol Beacon), which I mostly spent agog at the chaotic force of Pete'n'Carl at their peak. But in 2005, my on/off relationship with sound changed once more. Bundling into my parents' car with my friends after a particularly noisy gig, they chattered away as we drove home, enthusing about what they'd just seen. At least, I assume they did – because I couldn't hear them. The world had gone mute, my ears blasted from several hours in the front row. I nodded and smiled along with everyone, terrified my hearing might be permanently reduced. In the morning, things had barely improved; I was used to a bit of post-gig ringing in the ears, but this was different. Days went past, then weeks, and while my hearing returned to something approaching normal, the ringing remained. I went to the doctor, who confirmed I was suffering from tinnitus: an incurable, annoying, ever-present whine. The echoes of my early-years stereo mishap were undeniable – but this time my inner silence was gone, never to return. Just like the musicians in this book were beginning to realise, the time for quiet was over. I still miss it.

Further Listening

Alfie – *A Word in Your Ear* (Twisted Nerve Records, 2002)

Alfie – *Do You Imagine Things?* (Parlophone, 2003)

Alfie – *Crying at Teatime* (Regal, 2005)

Badly Drawn Boy – *It Came from the Ground* (Twisted Nerve Records, 1999)

Badly Drawn Boy – *About a Boy* (Twisted Nerve Records/XL, 2002)

Badly Drawn Boy – *Have You Fed the Fish?* (Twisted Nerve Records/XL, 2002)

Coldplay – *The Blue Room EP* (Parlophone, 1999)

Coldplay – *A Rush of Blood to the Head* (Parlophone, 2002)

Coldplay – *X&Y* (Parlophone, 2005)

Dido – *Life For Rent* (Arista, 2003)

Doves – *The Last Broadcast* (Heavenly Recordings, 2002)

Doves – *Lost Sides* (Heavenly Recordings, 2003)

Doves – *Some Cities* (Heavenly Recordings, 2005)

Elbow – *Cast of Thousands* (V2, 2003)

Elbow – *Leaders of the Free World* (V2, 2005)

Elbow – *The Seldom Seen Kid* (Fiction/Polydor, 2008)

Elbow – *Dead in the Boot* (Fiction/Polydor, 2012)

The Electric Soft Parade – *The American Adventure* (BMG, 2003)

The Electric Soft Parade – *The Human Body EP* (Truck, 2005)

The Electric Soft Parade – *No Need To Be Downhearted* (Truck, 2007)

David Gray – *Sell, Sell, Sell* (EMI, 1996)

David Gray – *Lost Songs 95-98* (iht/EastWest, 2001)

David Gray – *A New Day At Midnight* (iht/EastWest, 2002)

David Gray – *Life in Slow Motion* (Atlantic, 2005)

Ed Harcourt – *Here be Monsters* (Heavenly Recordings, 2001)

Kings of Convenience – *Versus* (Source, 2001)

Kings of Convenience – *Riot on an Empty Street* (Source, 2004)

Kings of Convenience – *Declaration of Dependence* (Source, 2009)

Lowgold – *Welcome to Winners* (Sanctuary, 2003)

Lowgold – *Keep Music Miserable* (DedTed, 2005)

Lowgold – *Promise Lands* (Cooking Vinyl, 2008)

Mull Historical Society – *Us* (Blanco Y Negro, 2003)

Mull Historical Society – *This is Hope* (B-Unique, 2004)

Colin MacIntyre – *The Water* (Pinnacle, 2007)

Tom McRae – *Tom McRae* (DB Records, 2000)

Tom McRae – *Just Like Blood* (DB Records, 2003)

Erlend Øye – *Unrest* (Source, 2003)

Snow Patrol – *Songs for Polarbears* (Jeepster, 1998)

Snow Patrol – *Final Straw* (Fiction, 2003)

Snow Patrol – *Eyes Open* (Fiction, 2006)

Starsailor – *Love is Here* (Chrysalis, 2001)

Travis – *Good Feeling* (Independiente, 1997)

Travis – *The Invisible Band* (Independiente, 2001)

Travis – *12 Memories* (Independiente, 2003)

Turin Brakes – *The Door EP* (Anvil, 1999)

Turin Brakes – *Ether Song* (Source, 2003)

Kathryn Williams – *Dog Leap Stairs* (Caw Records, 1999)

Kathryn Williams – *Old Low Light* (Caw Records, 2002)

Kathryn Williams – *Relations* (Caw Records, 2004)

Various Artists – *Acoustic.* (V2/Echo, 2002)

Various Artists – *Acoustic 2* (V2/Echo, 2002)

Various Artists – *Acoustic 3* (V2/Echo, 2003)

Various Artists – *Acoustic 4* (V2/Echo, 2004)

Various Artists – *Acoustic 5* (V2/Echo, 2005)

Various Artists – NME *in Association with War Child Presents 1 Love* (B-Unique, 2002)

Endnotes

Quotes are largely referenced within the body of the text, but there are a few which require a credit or source. They are listed here.

Statistics from the Millennium Bug section are sourced from Britannica.com. 'Disruptions...' quote, and that of John Koskinen, from a *New York Times* article on the upcoming millennium.

'A year ago today...' is sourced from footage of Travis' 1999 Glastonbury performance, shown here: www.youtube.com/watch?v=Os853AL-Ihw

Fran Healy's 'shit on a digestive' quote is from an interview with *Spin* in December 1997.

'with the sole intention...' and 'I'm beginning to realise...' are both from *Closer Every Year: The Story of Travis* by Mike Black (Independent Music Press, 2000), ps. 28 & 61 respectively.

Fran Healy's quote 'It was like supporting the Rolling Stones...' is from an *NME* interview in 2018.

Dougie Payne's quote, 'we recorded it over six months...' is from the press release for *The Man Who*, archived here: http://forum.travisonline.com/band/?id=21&p=20

Fran Healy's quote 'an album for staying in rather that going out' and Dougie Payne's 'If there's an underlying theme...' are both from *Closer Every Year: The Story of Travis* by Mike Black (Independent Music Press, 2000), p.81.

'We all thought it was a really below-par performance...' is from an interview with *Clash* magazine in April 2019.

'I haemorrhaged confidence in the political system...' is from an interview with the *Financial Times* in March 2016.

'Could not think of two more different approaches', and 'There is no one up there...' are both sourced from *Travis: The Man Who at 20* (BBC Scotland, 2019).

David Gray's quote 'I can think of no greater moment of inspiration...' is from *David Gray: A Biography* by Michael Heatley (Omnibus Press, 2001), p.10.

Dave Anderson's quote, 'I don't think the label knew what to do with it...' is from *David Gray: A Biography* by Michael Heatley (Omnibus Press, 2001), p.26.

David Gray's quote 'a few posters went up...' is from *David Gray: A Biography* by Michael Heatley (Omnibus Press, 2001), p.44.

Dave Matthews's quote 'When we first heard *White Ladder*...' is taken from YouTube footage of him discussing the album, shown here: www.youtube.com/watch?v=ybcck34UHoE

David Gray's quote 'I've been a slow learner...' is from the interview with the *Irish Post* in July 2014, referenced later in the chapter.

Rollo Armstrong's quote beginning 'I'd been really lucky...' is from the *Guardian* profile of the Armstrongs, 'How Dido Did It', in May 2001

Dido's quote describing 'Here With Me' as a 'post-shag song' is from a *Guardian* interview with her in January 2001.

Paul Arthurs a.k.a. 'Bonehead's quote 'I always thought we should have bowed out after the second night at Knebworth' is from a *Guardian* profile of departing band members in June 2009.

The quote from an Oasis fan describing them as 'the greatest band in the world... since The Beatles' is sourced from a BBC report on *Be Here Now*'s release day, shown here: www.youtube.com/watch?v=Yw646zIEBD4

Dave Rofe's quote 'answering the phone if needed…' is taken from an email from Dave in July 2020.

Jeff Barrett's quote 'Rob incredibly sadly and prematurely passed away…' is from an interview on the PIAS website, celebrating 25 years of Heavenly Recordings.

Andy Williams's quote 'I had a book of short ghost stories…' is from a tweet about 'The Cedar Room' for Tim Burgess's *Lost Souls* Twitter Listening Party, April 2020.

Guy Garvey's quote 'I read somewhere…' is from an interview with *Free Williamsburg* in March 2002.

Damon Gough's quote 'a song cycle, really…' is from an interview with *Northern Soul* in February 2016.

'the burden of simply representing myself…' is from the 2010 *UK Music Reviews* interview referenced earlier in the chapter.

'I tend to come out with questions…' is from an interview with the *LA Times* in August 2002.

Chris Martin's quote 'Meeting Jonny…' is found in *Coldplay: Nobody Said It Was Easy* by Martin Roach (Omnibus Press, 2003), p.18.

Steve Lamacq's quote 'I go to a lot of gigs…' is found in *Going Deaf for a Living* by Steve Lamacq (Omnibus Press, 2019), p.223.

Jonny Buckland's quote 'We didn't have to do the acoustic thing…' is found in *Coldplay: Nobody Said It Was Easy* by Martin Roach (Omnibus Press, 2003), p.90.

Gary Lightbody's quote 'We went to Scotland to form a Northern Irish band' is from a Virgin Radio interview with Chris Evans in July 2019.

The 'overwhelming politeness' quote is from an *NME* review of *When It's All Over We Still Have To Clear Up* in 2001.

'We spent 10 years making records that 6000 people bought' is a quote from the promotional material for Snow Patrol's album *A Hundred Million Suns* (2008).

Broadband statistics taken from the article 'Broadband: The First Decade' by Kate Youde, *The Independent,* March 2010.

The 'mimsy Viking warlords of NAM' quote is from an *NME* review of the single 'Toxic Girl' in 2001.

Eirik Bøe's quote 'I'm still proud of the Afghanistan protest…' is from *Quiet is the New Loud* by Ørjan Nilsson (Falck Forlag AS, 2014), p.73.

The quote 'Go and see them play' is from an *NME* review of Turin Brakes at The Social, London, in 2000.

The quote 'staring down the spectre of bankruptcy' is from Lowgold's biography on their own site, www.lowgold.co.uk

Dan Symons's quote 'It wasn't really a conscious thing…' is taken from an interview with Andrew Mclean for isnakebite.com, 2000.

The quote from Nude Records regarding their liquidation is from the *NME*, December 2001.

Dan Symons's quote 'After everything we'd been through…' is from Lowgold's website.

The quote 'Frighteningly assured and self-aware… still the Brit siblings to watch' is from a *Guardian* review of *The American Adventure* from October 2003.

Gary Lightbody's quote, 'just assumed I'd be a rock'n'roll star', is from a *Guardian* profile of Snow Patrol in April 2006.

The quote about Kathryn Williams's *Hypoxia* beginning 'Plath's work and life…' is taken from an *Irish Times* review of the album in June 2015.

Dan Symons's quote 'That, as far as we were concerned, was the end of it…' is taken from the band's biography on the archived Lowgold website. The quote beginning 'The trio know…' is from the same source.

Colin MacIntyre's quote beginning 'Those three albums taught me that less is more…' is from a *Guardian* profile of him in July 2004.

The 'octopus-on-crack drumming…' quote is from an *NME* review of 'If That's the Case, Then I Don't Know' from April 2007.

Bibliography

Black, Mike *Closer Every Year: The Story of Travis* (Independent Music Press, 2000)

Edgerton, David *The Rise and Fall of the British Nation: A Twentieth Century History* (Penguin, 2018)

Ellingham, Mark & Buckley, Jonathan (eds.) *The Rough Guide to Rock* (Rough Guides, Updated 2nd ed. 1999)

Goodman, Lizzy *Meet Me in the Bathroom: Rebirth and Rock'n'Roll in New York City 2001-2011* (Faber & Faber, 2017)

Hancox, Dan *Inner City Pressure: The Story of Grime* (William Collins, 2018)

Harris, John *The Last Party: Britpop, Blair and the Demise of English Rock* (Harper Perennial, 2004)

Heatley, Michael *David Gray: A Biography* (Omnibus Press, 2001)

Jenkins, Simon *A Short History of England* (Profile, 2018)

Lamacq, Steve *Going Deaf for a Living* (Omnibus Press, 2019)

MacIntyre, Colin & Macaskill, Ellen *Hometown Tales: Highlands and Hebrides* (Weidenfeld & Nicolson, 2018)

MacIntyre, Colin *The Letters of Ivor Punch* (Weidenfeld & Nicolson, 2016)

Middles, Mick *Reluctant Heroes: The Story of Elbow* (Omnibus Press, 2009)

Nilsson, Ørjan (trans. Holden, Paul) *Quiet is the New Loud* (Falck Forlag AS, 2014)

Odell, Jenny *How to do Nothing: Resisting the Attention Economy* (Melville House Publishing, 2019)

Rachel, Daniel *Don't Look Back in Anger: The Rise and Fall of Cool Britannia, Told by Those Who Were There* (Trapeze, 2019)

Reynolds, Simon *Retromania: Pop Culture's Addiction to its Own Past* (Faber & Faber, 2011)

Roach, Michael *Coldplay: Nobody Said it Was Easy* (Omnibus Press, 2003)

Roberts, David (ed.) *British Hit Singles and Albums, Vol. 19* (Guinness World Records, 2006)

Stubbs, David *1996 & The End of History* (Repeater Books, 2016)

Toop, David *Ocean of Sound: Ambient Sound and Radical Listening in the Age of Communication* (Serpent's Tail, 2018)

Wild, Debs & Croft, Malcolm *Life in Technicolour: A Celebration of Coldplay* (Carlton Books, 2018)

Online resources: *NME, The Guardian, Financial Times, Drowned in Sound, Uncut, Mojo, Q, The Quietus, The Scotsman, Shaking Through, Pitchfork, Free Williamsburg, The Times, Werk.Re, The Independent, The Telegraph, The Northampton Chronicle, All Music, Pop Matters, Travis Online, Spin, Discogs, Magnet, Belfast Telegraph, UK Music Reviews, Rock's Back Pages, The Great Rock Bible, Ether Site, Doves Music Blog, Musicweek, Songwriting Magazine*

All chart data taken from OfficialCharts. com

Acknowledgements

My father passed away in October 2020. This book is dedicated to his memory.

I'd like to thank all the musicians featured here – without you, this book simply would not exist. Next, those who kindly gave up their time for interviews or to otherwise help bring the story to life: Eirik Glambek Bøe, Darren Ford, Lee Gorton, Fran Healy, Olly Knights, Colin MacIntyre, Tom McRae, Gale Paridjanian, Dave Rofe, Dan Symons, Andy Votel, Thomas White, Alex White, Debs Wild, Andy Williams and Kathryn Williams.

I'm eternally grateful to Ian Daley at Route for taking a chance on this project, and for his patience and wisdom in helping it reach the world. I'd also like to thank Oliver Primus at *The 405* and Derek Robertson at *Drowned in Sound* who first provided me with the space and opportunity to write about music.

Large parts of this book were written in Walthamstow Public Library. Support your local.

Special thanks to Michael Macfarlane, Jay Greaves, Sarah Wray and Angelique Neumann for their endless and steadfast reassurances – and to numerous other friends and family members who have helped me along the way. I love you all.

The biggest thank you in this book is reserved for Robyn, who bravely put up with me writing it.

Tom Clayton is a writer whose non-fiction has appeared in *The Sunday Times*, *Drowned in Sound*, *Louder Than War* and *The 405*, and whose fiction has appeared in *The Santa Fe Literary Review*.

He was the lead researcher and writer for *Messing Up the Paintwork: The Wit and Wisdom of Mark E. Smith* (Ebury, 2018); *When Quiet Was the New Loud* is his first original book.

He lives and works in east London.

For more information on this book,
plus Route's full list of books, please visit:

www.route-online.com